MARXISM AND DEMOCRACY

MARXISM AND DEMOCRACY

edited and introduced

by

ALAN HUNT

LAWRENCE AND WISHART
LONDON

Lawrence and Wishart Ltd
39 Museum Street
London WC1

First published 1980
Copyright © Lawrence and Wishart, 1980
ISBN 85315 531 3

*Printed and bound in Great Britain at
The Camelot Press Ltd, Southampton*

CONTENTS

These papers were first presented under the title of 'Marxism and Democracy' at a conference in December 1978 organized by the Sociology Group of the Communist Party of Great Britain. They have been revised by the authors and an introduction has been added.

INTRODUCTION: TAKING DEMOCRACY SERIOUSLY

Alan Hunt

The suggestion that democracy should be taken seriously has a deliberately polemical intent. It poses the suggestion that socialists and Marxists can be charged with failing to take democracy seriously, and that this is not just a problem of the responsibility of socialists of an earlier period but that it is a current problem which we ignore at our peril. But if this charge is to be made, it is advanced not to convict others (or to exonerate ourselves) but to assist in clarifying the nature of the 'problem of democracy'.

The charge of failing to take democracy seriously is many-sided. For example, it includes the suggestion that the early attempts to elaborate a strategy for the transition to socialism under the conditions of bourgeois democracy were gestures which made tacit recognition of questions of political democracy, within a basic strategy that remained insurrectionary – even though the insurrection was seen as electoral rather than military. But the charge also raises the question of whether the theoretical framework of Marxism, especially in its most potent form developed by Lenin, has been adequate to the task of confronting 'the problem of democracy'.

The issues posed are ones which necessarily move between the two key areas of Marxist theory and socialist strategy. The questions posed are theoretical but have immediate political ramifications; the political questions depend upon and raise basic issues for Marxist theory. This essay seeks on the one hand to raise some general issues which constitute barriers towards taking democracy seriously and, on the other, to raise those which take the discussion of democracy further. It is hoped that this discussion will lay a basis for the more detailed papers which follow.

It is necessary to start by setting out the scope of the present discussion. The papers collected in this volume take as their focus the problem of bourgeois democracy, or the democratic forms, institutions and practices that are to be found predominantly in the advanced capitalism of Western Europe and North America. As a consequence the discussion does not seek to grapple with questions concerning socialist democracy. Yet it must be insisted that the question of socialist democracy is not one totally removed from the problem of bourgeois democracy. In the most minimal sense the nature of the transition to socialism, and the specific levels and forms of democratic practices involved, have profound ramifications on the subsequent development of socialist democracy. Yet it is necessary to insist that the discussion of socialist democracy raises a distinct and therefore separate range of issues, which would necessarily involve issues such as the nature of the socialist mode of production as well as the historical experience of 'real socialism'. The analysis and discussion of these problems is in its early stages of development; until these debates have been more thoroughly developed, Marxists tend to be restricted to a combination of responses to particular developments and a much deeper disquiet and even revulsion at the practice of socialist democracy under conditions of 'real socialism'. However important these questions, they are not the focus of this work.

What is essential for the discussion of the 'problem of democracy' is to find the appropriate starting-point. All Marxists will readily agree that this starting-point cannot be any notion of 'democracy in general'. But the alternative to a discussion of democracy in the abstract is often presented as the need for a *class analysis* of democracy. Nowhere is this more powerfully expressed than in Lenin's polemic against Kautsky in 'The Proletarian Revolution and the Renegade Kautsky' (*Collected Works*, vol. 28, p. 227).

It is natural for a liberal to speak of 'democracy' in general; but a Marxist will never forget to ask: 'for what class?' (ibid., 235).

Here we encounter what is perhaps the most basic or fundamental problem that underlies the 'problem of democracy'. Lenin's position involves much more than the contention that there is a definite historical association between the dominance of particular classes and the associated political forms of that rule. Lenin himself stresses that this is not a simple or direct relationship, since the rule of a class can take a wide range of political forms. Thus capitalist rule has manifested itself in a wide range of political forms including monarchical, fascist and parliamentary democratic systems. Yet Lenin goes further when he poses

the question of 'democracy for what class?'. This can only carry the
implication that the specific historical forms of democracy constitute
democracy for a specific class or classes and the denial of democracy for
other classes. Thus, for example, the democracy of slave cities and states
was democracy for the slave owners and dictatorship over the slaves
(ibid., p. 235). With this there is no dispute, but it evades the problem of
bourgeois democracy since bourgeois democracy's precise significance is
the inclusion *within* the democratic framework of the dominated classes.

Nor are the problems posed by Lenin's position resolved by reference
to the importance which he attached to the working class taking the
maximum possible advantages offered by bourgeois democracy.[1]* This
insistence is undoubtedly important but it neither contradicts nor even
modifies the central thesis that bourgeois democracy is democracy for
the capitalist class and the denial of democracy for the working class.
It follows that for Lenin the transition from capitalism to socialism
necessarily involves the transition from one political form of class rule to
another political form of class rule: parliamentary democracy superseded
by soviets.[2]

It is necessary now to add to this the theory of the state elaborated by
Lenin in *State and Revolution*: All states are machines for the
suppression of one class by another, hence the creation of the form of
state appropriate to the rule of the proletariat requires the destruction of
the bourgeois state and the construction of a new proletarian (the soviet)
state.

Lenin, his writings and revolutionary practice, has provided the central
and inescapable point of reference for all discussions of the state and
democracy; his *State and Revolution* and the polemic against Kautsky
have been the central points of reference. Many of the most important
discussions since 1917 take Lenin as their starting-point; this was the
case in the immediate aftermath of October 1917 in the writings of Karl
Kautsky and Rosa Luxemburg and then Antonio Gramsci, and remains
true of the modern writings of Louis Althusser and Nicos Poulantzas.

At the core of the issues raised by Lenin lies a fundamental theoretical
issue: the nature of the relationship between economics and politics.
Lenin advanced a strict relationship between stages of economic
development and their associated forms of the state. For the purposes of
our discussion this can be presented in the following form:

*See notes at end of each article.

Economic/class stage	Form of state
Capitalism	Bourgeois/parliamentary democracy
Socialism	Dictatorship of the proletariat

This analysis also takes a more detailed form in Lenin's writings, specifically arising in *State and Revolution*.

Mode of production	Form of state
Capitalism	Parliamentary democracy
Monopoly capitalism	'Bureaucratic-military state'
Socialism	Dictatorship of the proletariat

This presentation which emphasizes monopoly capitalism as a distinct stage of the capitalist mode of production, having a distinct state form, has played an important part in the discussion in recent decades of the possibilities of non-insurrectionary or 'peaceful' roads to socialism. For the moment we should note that Lenin does not go very far in analysing the nature of the associated state form; the emphasis on the bureaucratic-military tendency remains essentially descriptive. The general characterization is not in doubt; the general character is authoritarian producing a state form which comes more and more into conflict with parliamentary democracy which may be retained as the constitutional form. This stage Lenin sees as uniting the major combatants of the 1914–1918 war.

We can return for the time being to consider the more basic 'class theory' which presents capitalist and socialist societies as being characterized by specific general forms of the state: parliamentary democracy *vs* the dictatorship of the proletariat. It is important to recognize that there are present in Lenin's argument elements which develop this framework by seeking to identify sub-stages but which do nothing to alter the basic or essential features of the analysis: the political form is derived from and determined by the economic stage or level of development.

It is not the purpose of this essay to discuss the general theoretical issue on which Lenin's analysis is based. I do not intend to discuss the general theory of the relationship between 'politics' and 'economics'. It is sufficient to note that the main theoretical thrust in recent years, taking a variety of different forms, has been to propose a theory of the 'relative autonomy' of politics from economics. Such a position drawing on textual authority present in the writings of Marx and particularly Engels,[3] and also occurring in Lenin, posits that politics are not directly determined by the economy, but that the determinacy of the economic is only true 'in the final analysis'. This general position underlies such diverse positions as those of Gramsci, Althusser, Poulantzas and Ralph Miliband, to cite only a few. It should be noted that more recently the very possibility of developing a coherent theory of 'relative autonomy' has been challenged. This thrust has come in particular from Barry Hindess and Paul Hirst, and a general statement of the position occurs in Hindess's essay in this book.

Without entering into this perhaps most basic theoretical problem confronting contemporary Marxism, one comment on the current discussion appears necessary. How is the challenge to central aspects in the existing state of Marxist theory to be responded to? The most dangerous response, and there are indications that it is a common one, is to react defensively, to protect 'Marxist orthodoxy', and thereby fail to take issue with the challenging theoretical and political problems posed.[4]

My focus will be upon a number of issues which, while related to the general problem of the relationship between economics and politics, centre more directly on the question of democracy. The core issues upon which an assessment of Lenin's theory rest are:

(i) the extent to which bourgeois democracy is to be evaluated as democracy for the bourgeoisie and denial of democracy to the working class;

(ii) the assessment of the theory of the revolutionary transition from capitalism to socialism which requires the destruction of an existing state form as appropriate to the rule of one class, and the construction of another state expressing the requirements of the working class as the new ruling class.

Let us first consider the nature of bourgeois democracy, or more specifically of parliamentary democracy. Its distinctive characteristics are twofold: first the universalization of the political franchise (it being noted that this process occurs unevenly and over a relatively prolonged period of time) and, second, the system of political competition.

To what extent does the extension of the franchise, the development of worker's parties and the numerical growth of wage workers to a massive majority of the population affect Lenin's insistence that parliamentary democracy is democracy *for* the capitalist class? Lenin himself takes on this question when he argues that class dictatorship involves

the abolition (or very material restriction, which is also a form of abolition) of democracy for the class over which, or against which, the dictatorship is exercised (cw, vol. 28, p. 235).

The problematic feature is whether 'restriction' of democracy for a class can be regarded as 'abolition' of democracy for a class. There is no argument that parliamentary democracy operates with many real and important 'restrictions' that affect the subordinate classes: the wealth of dominant parties, and unequal control over and access to the media are only two of these restrictions. But under conditions of what I will call for the moment 'normal' bourgeois democracy, while the conditions of political competition are never equal, they cannot be said to constitute an abolition of democracy. Indeed there are certain respects in which working-class parties may have specific advantages; for example, it seems incontestable that in Britain the specific relationship between trade unions and the Labour Party has been and remains a very considerable asset to the latter.

The specific form taken by parliamentary democracy needs to be considered. It is argued that bourgeois democracy operates in such a way that populations and classes are atomized as 'citizens'. The citizens stand equal before the ballot-box however unequal all their other conditions of social life may be. From a similar base it may be argued that the geographical constituency deals with the citizens as residents, in contrast to the more collective conditions of the work situations of the majority of workers. Further, parliamentary democracies achieve the election not of delegates from the electorate but representatives largely uncontrollable and unrecallable by their constituents. But beyond the political limits of bourgeois democracy is the insistence that the coexistence of private property and wage slavery strips away the formal equality of bourgeois democracy to reveal the absence of democracy and the continuing dictatorship of the bourgeoisie.

It is now possible to understand more clearly Lenin's insistence, referred to previously, on the importance of the proletariat making use of all the possibilities of bourgeois democracy and legality. His conception is contained within the objective of encouraging the autonomous development of a revolutionary worker's movement. The objective of this development is the achievement of a stage of maturity of the revolutionary movement in which it is able to pass beyond bourgeois democracy, stripped of any illusions, to the conquest of political power, in so doing smashing bourgeois democracy as a necessary precursor to the establishment of the 'new' state, the dictatorship of the proletariat.

What is absent from Lenin is any recognition of the contradictory character of bourgeois democracy. The element is found in a developed form in Marx's discussion of the bourgeois democratic republic in *Class Struggles in France*:

The comprehensive contradiction of this constitution, however, consists in the following: The classes whose social slavery the constitution is to perpetuate, proletariat, peasantry, petty bourgeoisie, it puts in possession of political power through universal suffrage. And from the class whose old social power it sanctions, the bourgeoisie, it withdraws the political guarantees of this power. It forces the political rule of the bourgeoisie into democratic conditions, which at every moment help the hostile classes to victory and jeopardise the very foundations of bourgeois society (Marx/Engels, *Selected Works in Three Volumes*, vol. 1, pp. 235–6).

It is this aspect which Engels, however, treats in a rather mechanical manner in his well-known 1895 *Introduction* to this work in which he develops the scenario of an uninterrupted progress to socialism through the expansion of the votes of the German Social Democratic Party. Yet Lenin completely evades the contradictory possibilities of bourgeois democracy and the franchise.

This treatment of bourgeois democracy is reinforced by the additional element stemming from Lenin's analysis of monopoly capitalism and imperialism. More and more insistently does he argue after 1914 that the rise of monopoly capitalism results in the demise of bourgeois democracy and produces the more or less rapid degeneration into political reaction and authoritarianism.

The political superstructure of this new economy, of monopoly capitalism (imperialism is monopoly capitalism) is the change *from* democracy *to* political reaction. Democracy corresponds to free competition. Political reaction corresponds to monopoly (CW, vol. 23, p. 43).

During the same period, looking at the states participating in the imperialist war, he came more and more frequently to deny the significance of differences in the political framework within which this demise of bourgeois democracy manifested itself. As a consequence, the analysis of bourgeois democracy is no longer for Lenin a pressing, current problem, but a past which has been historically overtaken by the onward march of monopoly capitalism.

It must be recognized that at a number of levels Lenin was wrong in his analysis of the political consequences of the development of monopoly capitalism. First, grave reservations must be entered against the derivation of general laws of correspondence between economic stages and associated political or state forms. Second, Lenin is wrong in taking the evidence from a specific historical conjuncture, namely the inter-imperialist competition resulting in the 1914–1918 war, as evidence from which a general law of the transition from bourgeois democracy to reaction can be deduced. For however much from the vantage point of 1916 such a trend to reaction might seem to exist, the whole subsequent development of capitalism throughout the remainder of the twentieth century reveals the falsity of Lenin's theses.

The significant general feature of this period has been that monopoly capitalism has been most persistently successful and stable when associated with the preservation of bourgeois democratic forms. The general economic and political victory has gone to capitalist regimes that have preserved, and even expanded, bourgeois democracy. Even the dark period of the 1930s and 1940s, with the threat of the triumph of political reaction in the specific form of fascism, reveal the long-run triumph of bourgeois democracy, epitomized in the American New Deal and the British Welfare State.

None of this denies the existence of an ever-present contradiction within capitalist rule which under specific conditions exhibits tendencies to fulfil Lenin's thesis of the lurch to political reaction; this remains a persistent danger. Yet the characteristic state form of contemporary capitalist societies, with the current trends to state authoritarianism so well revealed in the recent work of Nicos Poulantzas and Stuart Hall,[5] nevertheless remains a tendency *within* bourgeois democracy.

It follows that bourgeois democracy is not a question of the past, but a very pressing contemporary question for socialists and Marxists. It is relatively simple to engage in a critique of the limitations, distortion and manipulation of democracy. Yet the much more fundamental question is to consider the potentialities, and their limits, for the transformation of bourgeois democracy. It is this theme embodied in the idea of the 'expansion' of democracy and drawing heavily on Gramsci that is the focus of the chapters by Anne Sassoon and Colin Mercer. Central to these questions are the extent to which popular struggle can operate to overcome the formal, and therefore limited, character of bourgeois democracy. Can the presence and action of popular forces qualitatively transform democratic practices? Can the result be that rather than bourgeois democracy operating formally to admit the masses whilst excluding them in practice, it can be compelled to yield an expanding arena of popular power?

A theme which is present in all the chapters revolves around the question of direct or popular democracy. Basic to this theme is that direct democracy is at one and the same time the self-activity of the masses, and a break on the formalist or incorporationist tendencies within bourgeois democracy. There is an important parallel with Lenin; his counter-opposition of bourgeois and direct democracy was the expression of two state forms (constituent assembly *vs* dictatorship of the proletariat). The counter-opposition in the tradition of Gramsci is not the opposition between state forms but the struggle for hegemony that is fought out prior to the transformation of state power itself.

We can thus perhaps see more readily the source of a serious problem in Lenin's treatment of bourgeois democracy. His insistence that 'democracy is a form of the state' (CW, vol. 25, p. 472) illegitimately conflates state and politics; the two become synonomous, with the result that politics, as well as the state, is the bearer of necessary and inevitable class essence. The Gramscian challenge to the Leninist tradition seeks to grapple with the specific character of 'politics', not itself reducible to the state. It is through politics that classes and social forces engage in struggle; as a consequence changes in the balance or relation of political forces themselves have consequences for the state and allow for the possibility of political strategies that have as their objective the transformation of the state. In this respect therefore transformation of the state replaces Lenin's idea of struggle between state forms, the present capitalist and the future workers' state existing in embryo; it was this conception that made it possible for Lenin readily to adopt the concept of 'dual power' as novel, though consistent with his analysis of the state.

The insistence on the need to distinguish politics and the state has a further important consequence. If the two are not reducible one to the other, it follows that politics and political struggle cannot be viewed as revolving exclusively around the goal of state power. It follows that specific forms of political practice do not carry an automatic or necessary class characteristic. Specific forms of political action may be regarded as particularly well adapted to the interest of specific political forces. For example, the strike is particularly suited to labour organization because of the forms of organization that are consequent upon the concentration of wage-labourers in the enterprise; but, as the Chilean lorry-owners showed in 1973, workers have no monopoly over strike action.

Forms of democratic action and organization do not carry an automatic class label. There is nothing specifically 'bourgeois' about parliamentary elections. Nor can they be counterposed to a system of recallable delegates as the essence of proletarian democracy. The class consequences of particular forms of democratic practices are only the result of the balance of forces at the specific time. Parliamentary democracy is thus bourgeois only in the sense that historically it has existed under conditions in which the bourgeoisie has been the hegemonic class.

The significance of this line of argument becomes sharper if we consider its impact on specific forms of democratic practice. One persistent feature of bourgeois democracy has been the importance attached to *political competition* whose most common form has been the competition of political parties. From the reduction by Lenin of democracy to forms of the state, it follows that political competition is a characteristic of the bourgeois state and is regarded as playing no necessary part in the workers' state. It need hardly be stressed that this conclusion has profound consequences for the development of the 'real socialism' of Eastern Europe.

The implication of this consideration of political competition is that it is a necessary element of democratic practice. But is this a retreat into 'democracy in general'? It is not such a retreat if we further examine the nature of the relationship between the historical stage embodied in the transition from capitalism to socialism. We need to guard against the evolutionary language that we are forced to use. But with this consideration in mind it is necessary to stress Marx's insistence that capitalism represented a major historical advance over earlier class societies since, in the economic and political developments it engendered, it laid the basis for the realization of a much higher stage of human freedom.

The project of socialist revolution must be seen as the completion, as against the destruction, of the historical stage initiated by the advent of capitalism; the essential condition of this advance is the removal of impediments imposed by the specifically capitalist organization of economic and social life. It follows that the sphere of democracy, which concerns the extension of human control over the social conditions of existence, lays down elements which have to be liberated from their limitation and distortion under capitalism. The project of socialism has as its goal the completion or realization of the democratic project initiated by the bourgeois revolutions of the eighteenth and nineteenth centuries. Although often presented as goals in their own right, nationalization and collectivism are means in the realization of the democratic project. Thus the realization of democracy involves not the smashing of bourgeois democracy but its completion, liberated from the undemocratic framework of capitalist relations. Political competition, representative government, political rights do not bear an ahistorical capitalist essence but provide elements whose transformation makes possible the attainment of the socialist project.

The transformation of bourgeois democracy should not be seen as a process that occurs only *after* the moment of revolution. Rather its transformation lies at the centre of the struggle for socialism; hence the expansion of the sphere of democracy is an integral and even central feature of class struggle under capitalism. These considerations have important political ramifications which need to act as a corrective to the highly economistic view of the struggle for socialism that has dominated both the communist and non-communist left in Britain since 1917. Although the specific forms of political strategy exhibit considerable variation, the basic content shows remarkable continuity. Central has been the conception of the task of socialist revolution as being to develop the contradiction between the capitalist and working class to the point at which the taking of state power becomes possible. The immediate tasks of working-class political power have been seen as the expropriation of the capitalist class through nationalization of industrial and financial capital. The development of a political superstructure has received very little attention, and the development of popular or proletarian democracy has been regarded very much as something to be developed *after* the completion of the main tasks of revolutionary transformation.

A political perspective which emphasizes the necessity and possibility of the expansion of democracy as a precondition of socialist advance requires a radically different view of socialist strategy. First it necessitates a changed strategy of alliances in which the problem is no longer how other classes, for example the petty bourgeoisie or the peasantry, are to be limited as subordinate partners to the working class. If classes are not seen as homogenous entities it follows that political forces do not bear a direct or necessary relationship to classes. It is in this context that Bob Jessop takes up and explores that tantalizing and often rhetorical concept of 'the people'. Building upon a tradition of work in which Ernesto Laclau has made an important contribution, he explores the conditions for what he tentatively (and perhaps not too elegantly) calls 'people formation'. His major thrust is to argue that the conditions for democracy are not only formal but are also political. Without the presence of a strong and active 'people' as a popular force in opposition to the state, there can be no democracy.

The limitations of democracy within capitalist society stem from its primarily formal characteristics. The major thrust of the argument advanced in this collection is that this is not an absolute barrier. Rather a major feature of current socialist strategy must be to intervene with respect to the limits and possibilities of democracy to realize an expansion of democracy as a precondition for the realization of socialism. This requires that we take democracy seriously in a way that has been impeded by the counter-posing of bourgeois and proletarian democracy in the tradition of Lenin.

NOTES

1. See for example, 'Two Tactics of Social Democracy', *Collected Works* (CW), vol. 9; 'The Democratic Tasks of the Revolutionary Proletariat', CW, vol. 8; 'Reply to P. Kievsky', CW, vol. 23; and 'A Caricature of Marxism', ibid.
2. It is perhaps worthwhile noting that as late as 1915 this counterposition of parliament *vs.* soviets was much less sharp; indeed Lenin still took the democratic republic as general objective: 'The political form of a society wherein the proletariat is victorious in overthrowing the bourgeoisie will be a democratic republic' ('On the Slogan for a United States of Europe', CW, vol. 21, p. 342).
3. See in particular the letter of Engels to Bloch (21/9/1890), Schmidt (27/10/1890), Mehring (14/7/1893) and Starkenburg [Borgius] (25/1/1894) in *Marx-Engels Selected Correspondence*, Lawrence and Wishart, 1960.

4. I cite, as one recent example of this failure, Mike Bleaney's review of Cutler, Hindess, Hirst and Hussain, 'Marx's Capital and Capitalism Today', in *Marxism Today*, September 1978.
5. Nicos Poulantzas, *State, Power, Socialism*, NLB, Stuart Hall *et al.*, *Policing the Crisis*, Macmillan, 1978.

MARXISM AND PARLIAMENTARY DEMOCRACY

Barry Hindess

In his Introduction to Marx's *The Class Struggles in France*, Engels celebrates the new methods of struggle developed by the German working class in making use of universal suffrage. Compared with other political systems, he argues, those based on universal suffrage have one inestimable advantage:

> that it accurately informed us concerning our own strength and that of all hostile parties, and thereby provided us with a measure of proportion for our actions second to none, safeguarding us from untimely timidity as much as from untimely foolhardiness (Marx/Engels, *Selected Works in One Volume* (MESW), p. 660)*.

The machinery of the parliamentary state provides the working class with a weapon to use against the state and the class it represents.

> And so it happened that the bourgeoisie and the government came to be much more afraid of the legal than of the illegal action of the workers' party, of the results of elections than of those of rebellion (ibid.).

This new method of struggle, the mass party organized as an electoral force, has largely superseded the old-style methods of street fighting and the like. So:

> if *we* are not so crazy as to let ourselves be driven to street fighting in order to please them, then in the end there is nothing left for them to do but themselves break through this fatal legality (ibid., p. 666).

At the time he was writing, and ever since, the representative institutions of parliamentary democracy have posed severe problems for Marxist theory that have never been satisfactorily resolved, problems of political analysis, of the characterization of arenas of struggle and the forces engaged in them, problems of democratic theory, and problems concerning the movement from capitalism to socialism. The weaknesses

* For full references see p. 54.

of Engels's argument are clear enough: he confuses voting for a party with support for its long-term objectives, and his conception of the movement of transformation from capitalism is most ambiguous. On the one hand he presents the prospect of a progressive shift in the balance of state power with the growing strength and organization of the working class, and on the other he writes of the need to preserve our forces against 'the decisive day' (ibid., p. 665), when other modes of struggle will presumably come to the fore. Thus his argument appears to invoke both a parliamentary-democratic and an insurrectionary transfer of power and, since the relationship between them remains unclear in Engels's account, it has been read as supporting the most diverse conceptions of the movement towards socialism.

The confusions and ambiguities of Engels's account have haunted subsequent Marxist discussion. This paper tries to clarify some of the points at issue by considering two of the most significant early debates on parliamentary democracy and socialism, concentrating on Kautsky's commentary on the Erfurt programme of German social democracy and Bernstein's critique, and on the debate between Lenin and Kautsky over the question of the 'dictatorship of the proletariat'. I shall be mainly concerned with arguments over democracy, and parliamentary democracy in particular, although there are several other important issues at stake in these disputes, for example, the theory of value, the agrarian question, laws of tendency, etc.

Following a preliminary exposition and commentary on the arguments of Bernstein, Kautsky and Lenin, I proceed to consider two sets of issues arising out of those arguments: first, disputes over the relationship between classes and their interests on the one hand and the institutional conditions and features of parliamentary democracy on the other, and second, questions of the analysis of politics under conditions of parliamentary democracy and some related questions of democratic theory. Many of the issues raised in these debates have been obscured by accounts which counterpose an orthodoxy to revisionisms. Indeed, there are important respects in which all three positions discussed here face similar problems, and some of their differences pose fundamental and unresolved problems both of political analysis and of democratic theory that must be addressed by socialists in advanced capitalist democracies. Where some of these questions have been discussed, albeit not satisfactorily, is in the non-Marxist literature of political theory and political science – but I shall not attempt to deal with that literature here.

Kautsky's book, *The Class Struggle* (hereafter, CS) is an extended commentary on the programme adopted by the German Social Democratic Party at its congress in Erfurt in 1891. It presents an analysis of the nature of capitalist society and its development and outlines the objectives of social democracy and the means by which they are to be realized. Kautsky argues that socialism is the inevitable product of capitalist development, because of the economic effects of that development and their political consequences. The economic tendencies of capitalism involve an increasing polarization, with the decline of the peasantry and urban petty bourgeoisies, the concentration of capitalist production, and the growth of the organized working class so that it finally encompasses a majority of the population. The political consequences follow from the irreconcilability of the interests of the proletariat and bourgeoisie:

> Sooner or later in every capitalist country the participation of the working class in politics must lead to the formation of an independent party, a labor party. . . . And, once formed, such a party must have for its purpose the conquest of the government in the interests of the class which it represents. Economic development will lead naturally to the accomplishment of this purpose (CS, p. 189).

The industrial struggle of the working class leads it to make political demands, for the freedom to organize and for the rights needed to make that effective, freedom of speech, of the press and assembly. 'These privileges are to the proletariat the prerequisites of life; they are the light and air of the labour movement' (ibid., p. 185). Nevertheless, Kautsky argues that the highest form of political struggle is not spontaneously developed by the working class, but requires a non-utopian, socialist consciousness which must be imported into the working-class struggle from without. Left to itself the working class would not develop beyond trade union consciousness. Kautsky argues that it is necessary for the working class to engage in parliamentary struggle, not only because of its effects on government but also because of what it does to the working class:

> This very participation of the proletariat proves to be the most effective means of shaking up the hitherto indifferent divisions of the proletariat and giving them hope and confidence. It is the most powerful lever that can be utilized to raise the

proletariat out of its economic, social and moral degradation. . . . Besides freedom of the press and the right to organize, the universal ballot is to be regarded as one of the conditions prerequisite to a sound development of the proletariat (ibid., p. 188).

The parliamentary struggle itself forges the political cohesion of the class.

As for the modern parliamentary state, Kautsky's argument is similar to that of many recent advocates of a democratic road to socialism. On the one hand the state is an instrument of the ruling class and on the other it is capable of transformation through parliamentary struggle. The state will never go further in relation to nationalization or any other measure than the interests of the ruling class demand. It 'will not cease to be a capitalist institution until the proletariat has become the ruling class' (ibid., p. 110). But, while the state works in the interests of the bourgeoisie, parliament allows the working class to influence government activity. Parliament 'ceases to be a mere tool in the hands of the bourgeoisie' (ibid., p. 188).

In fact the struggle of the working class should be directed both towards an increase in the power of parliament in the state and towards the increase in their own influence within parliament. In the last resort, he argues, the power of parliament depends 'on the energy and courage of the classes behind it and on the energy and courage of the classes on which its will is to be imposed' (ibid., p. 187). The growing strength and political maturity of the working class means that sooner or later it will obtain a parliamentary majority and the ability to make parliament the dominant element in the state. The socialist transformation is then just a matter of time:

If the working class did not make use of its mastery over the machinery of government to introduce the socialist system of production, the logic of events would finally call some such system into being – but only after a useless waste of energy and time (ibid., p. 191).

So, the socialist transformation of society can be achieved through a parliamentary majority backed by mass popular support. Kautsky has little to say about the process of taking power and, on the whole, he is content to say that, while the character of the revolution will depend on the circumstances in which it takes place, it need not be accompanied by violence or bloodshed. One thing however is clear, that socialism will be reached only through the political strength and unity of the working

class. Kautsky is resolutely opposed to any attempt at gaining power
through a broadly based alliance of the popular classes, the radical
[...] intelligentsia and petty-bourgeoisie. In his
[...] (Kautsky, 1899) Kautsky argues that
[...] gerous and unnecessary. The Social
[...] working class, but that need not prevent
[...] joining or lending it their support.
[...] not a problem, but if the party tried to
[...] se its unity and strength of purpose and
[...] or example, he argues that a party of the
[...] t remain on the terrain of existing forms
[...] lly with regard to individual private
[...] tion. But a party of the working class
[...] , struggle for the transformation of the
[...] anization.

For Kautsky, the construction of a political majority for socialism is
not a problem in the long run: the development of the capitalist economy
will ensure that the working class will be an overwhelming majority of the
population, and the experience of industrial, political and parliamentary
struggle will weld them into an unbeatable socialist political force. The
foundations of Kautsky's optimistic thesis that socialism is the inevitable
product of capitalist development are attacked by Bernstein in a well-
known series of articles and in his book, *Evolutionary Socialism*
(hereafter ES). Bernstein argues first against the alleged tendencies of
capitalist development invoked by the Erfurt programme: the peasantry
and the middle classes were not disappearing, small businesses were not
being eliminated and the industrial working class was far from being an
overwhelming majority of the population. That meant that, at least for
the foreseeable future, there would always be a substantial portion of the
population, neither bourgeois nor proletarian, whose politics could
crucially affect the chances of achieving any major socialist objective.
Secondly, even amongst the working class, the rapid growth in
membership and votes of social democracy did not necessarily indicate
any great desire for socialism. There are many reasons why workers
might vote for or join the social democrats without being committed to
socialism. Bernstein uses the example of Britain to argue that capitalist
industrial development does not necessarily lead to the growth of socialist
consciousness among the working class. Thirdly, he casts doubt on the
present capacity of the working class to take over the organization of

production. For example, citing the Webb's *Industrial Democracy*, he argues that producer cooperatives have made such a poor showing primarily because of the contradiction between their democratic character on the one hand and the need for differentiation of functions and subordination once the unit reaches a fairly modest size on the other. For any reasonably large unit of production cooperative management is impossible: 'it is simply impossible that the manager should be the employee of those he manages, that he should be dependent for his position on their favour and their bad temper' (ES, p. 119).

The implications of that part of Bernstein's argument for social democratic politics are clear. Rather than direct its politics towards the utopian goal of a fully socialist society the social democratic party should aim at practical and realizable objectives, at social changes leading in a broadly socialist direction. It was in this sense that he could write that the movement means everything for him and 'the final aim of socialism' is nothing. Furthermore, since capitalism is not working to produce an overwhelming political majority for socialism, the achievement of socialist objectives must depend on the construction of political alliances between social democrats and other parties. These implications are well known, although the character of the Marxist response to Bernstein's work, concentrating on the defence of Marxist theory or on Bernstein's epistemology, has tended to obscure the political point of his argument.

However, for our purposes it is more interesting to look at what Bernstein has to say about democracy. Notice first that he makes a clear demarcation between revolutionary and democratic roads to political power. Revolution may well be quicker in the removal of obstacles and the power of privilege but its strength lies in its destructiveness. Parliamentary struggle and constitutional legislation are 'best adapted to positive social-political work' (ES, p. 218). In a parliamentary democracy 'the appeal to a revolution by force becomes a meaningless phrase' (ibid.). Bernstein argues that the achievement of democracy, 'the formation of political and social organs of the democracy, is the indispensable preliminary condition to the realization of socialism' (ibid., p. 163). Indeed it is in support of that point that Bernstein quotes Marx's and Engels's well-known comment on the lessons of the Commune, namely, that the working class cannot simply take possession of the state machinery and set it in motion for their own ends' (ibid., p. 156). But the situation of social democracy is very different from that confronting the Communards in that liberal democratic forms of political organization already exist. They may be limited but they are capable of change and development. 'They do not need to be destroyed but only to be further developed' (ibid., p. 163).

Bernstein offers what he describes as a negative definition of democracy, as an absence of class government, if not necessarily the absence of classes. That definition, he says, rules out 'the oppression of the individual by the majority which is absolutely repugnant to the modern mind' (ibid., p. 142). The central element here is universal suffrage, since *in the long run* that ensures the subjection of the state to popular control. I emphasize 'in the long run' because Bernstein insists that suffrage is no immediate panacea:

The right to vote in a democracy makes its members virtually partners in the community, and this virtual partnership must in the end lead to real partnership. With the working class undeveloped in numbers and culture the general right to vote may long appear as the right to choose 'the butcher'; with the growing number and knowledge of the workers it is changed, however, into the implement by which to transform the representatives of the people from masters into real servants of the people (ibid., p. 144).

As an example of this process he cites the Prussian anti-socialist law and its subsequent repeal. Bismarck used universal suffrage as a tool but 'finally it compelled Bismarck to serve it as a tool' (ibid.).

It is precisely because of this conception of the potentialities of democracy that Bernstein objects to the phrase 'dictatorship of the proletariat'. In an era of parliamentary democracy talk of the need for a *dictatorship* is anachronistic, it belongs to 'a lower civilization' (ibid., p. 146). Far from being a dictatorship, socialism must be the self-organization of the people:

If democracy is not to exceed centralized absolutism in the breeding of bureaucracies, it must be built up on an elaborately organized self-government with a corresponding economic, personal responsibility of all the units of administration as well as of the adult citizens of the state (ibid., p. 155).

The need for democracy in this sense is what Bernstein takes to be the principal lesson of the Commune.

There are several issues raised by these arguments of Kautsky and Bernstein to which we shall return in the subsequent discussion. For the present, however, it is sufficient to note the similarity in their assessment of parliamentary democracy, both as a necessity for the political development of the working class and as an instrument of popular control over the state. To be sure, Kautsky insists in his debate with Bernstein that the 'suppression of the individual' is by no means uncommon in modern states and that it is disingenuous of Bernstein to claim that practice to be 'absolutely repugnant to the modern mind'. And he strongly objects to Bernstein's characterization of democracy as the absence of class domination. Modern democratic states show no hesitation in suppressing strikes, trades unions and other organizations of the working class when they can get away with it. So the existence of democratic forms by no means renders the need for working-class supremacy superfluous (Kautsky also doubts the democratic character of Bismarck's Prussia – but that is another story). Nevertheless, for all the polemical force of these points there is little to choose between them with regard to the potential power that a parliamentary democracy gives to a popular majority. This assessment of parliamentary democracy is one of the central issues in the dispute between Lenin and Kautsky, to which we now turn.

II. KAUTSKY AND LENIN

In this section I shall concentrate on the general argument over socialism and democracy in Kautsky's *The Dictatorship of the Proletariat* and Lenin's response to it, although the dispute between them over parliamentary democracy and the road to socialism can be found earlier – for example, in *The State and Revolution* where Lenin asks, apropos of Kautsky's replies to the revisionists: but where is the revolution? I shall not consider Kautsky's account of events in Russia after October or Lenin's attempts to show that it is a complete distortion. *The Dictatorship of the Proletariat* (hereafter DP) was written in 1918 as a direct attack on the practices of the Bolsheviks, criticizing both their seizure of power in the second revolution of 1917 and their 'dictatorial' method of government thereafter. What is at stake in Kautsky's view is the clash between 'two fundamentally distinct methods, that of democracy and that of dictatorship' (DP, p. 1). He argues that the method of dictatorship is based on fundamental errors, that it cannot lead to socialism and that the working class can and must gain power by democratic means. Democracy cannot be regarded simply as a means to the end of socialism, for that conception suggests that other means might sometimes be appropriate. Modern socialism means 'not merely social organization of production, but democratic organization of society as well'. For that reason socialism without democracy is unthinkable.

Kautsky's argument is concerned first to show that socialism can be reached through democratic means and secondly to demonstrate the effects of dictatorship. In this paper we are concerned mainly with the first of these, and with what Kautsky has to say about the nature of democratic politics. To show that socialism can be reached by democratic means, Kautsky repeats the argument of *The Class Struggle*. Socialism is the inevitable product of capitalist development, first because the economic tendencies work to produce a working class majority and secondly because the experience of economic and political struggle welds them into an overwhelming political majority for socialism. In this transition a parliamentary majority, backed by a determined popular majority, is sufficient to push through the socialist transformation of society. The only danger is that of a right-wing coup. But what that shows is precisely that the bourgeoisie have good reason to fear democracy – and therefore that the working class should defend it tooth and nail. In any case if the working class waits till it is strong enough to conquer power through democratic means, it would be extremely difficult for 'the capitalist dictatorship to manipulate the force necessary for the suppression of democracy' (DP, p. 9).

Where Kautsky does go beyond his earlier work is not so much in the general argument for a democratic road to socialism but rather in what he has to say about the character of democratic politics. Democracy means majority rule, but, unlike bureaucracy, it also means civil liberties and the protection of minorities. These last are crucial since they provide conditions for political organizations to work out alliances and differences in an open way and allow for changes in the party of government. We will come back to the notion of a plurality of parties later. For the moment notice Kautsky's hostility to bureaucracy. Bureaucratic rule leads to arbitrariness, the suppression of minorities and general social and economic stagnation.

It is, then, urgently necessary for the executive to be subjected to public criticism, for free organizations of citizens to counterbalance the power of the state, for self-government of municipalities and provinces to be established, for the power of law-making to be taken from the bureaucracy, and put under the control of a central assembly, freely chosen by the people, that is, a parliament. The control of government is the most important duty of parliament, and in this it can be replaced by no other institution. . . . The activities of the executive can only be supervised by another central body, and not by an unorganized and formless mass of people (DP, p. 26).

We shall see that Lenin evades this argument for a freely-elected central assembly. But notice two features of Kautsky's position: first, the claim that parliament is able to exercise effective control of government bureaucracy; and second, the way Kautsky opposes a central assembly on the one hand to 'an unorganized and formless mass of people' on the other, as if those exhausted the possibilities. I shall return to both these points.

Kautsky argues that no modern, i.e. capitalist, state can continue to withstand popular pressure for universal suffrage and that the struggle between classes for control of the state 'is especially manifested in the struggle over the character of parliament, that is, in the fight for the franchise' (DP, p. 27). Here Kautsky returns to the view that the class character of parliament is ultimately determined by the extent of the franchise.

The final point to notice in Kautsky's characterization of democratic politics concerns his distinction between parties and classes. In a democracy, classes may rule but parties govern: 'the strength of parties changes even quicker than the strength of classes, and it is parties which aspire to power in a democracy' (DP, p. 31). The discrepancy between the analysis of politics in terms of parties and analysis in terms of classes is covered first by an act of Marxist faith:

the abstract simplification of theory, although necessary to a clear understanding of realities is true only in the last resort, and between it and actualities there are many intervening factors (DP, p. 31).

Second, it is covered by the idea that parties 'represent' classes:

A party is not synonymous with a class, although it may, in the first place, represent a class interest. *One and the same class interest can be represented in very different ways*, by various tactical methods. . . . Above all the deciding factor is the position in relation to other classes and parties (ibid., emphasis added).

For example, the Liberals and Conservatives in England represent the same class interest but they try to serve it through different alliances, with the working classes in the one case and the landed classes in the other.

The problem here is that if parties are thought to lie at a different level of analysis from classes, political alliances must be conceived either as between class and class or between party and party, but not between a party on the one hand and classes on the other. In effect Kautsky deploys the all-too-common Marxist manoeuvre of giving parties an autonomy from classes with one hand and taking it away again with the other. It is precisely this sleight-of-hand that allows him to treat the electoral strength of a party as a measure of the strength of a class. The advantage of democracy for the working class is that it 'gives a clear indication of the relative strength of classes and parties [sic]', whereas, under absolutism, 'the ruling, as well as the revolutionary, classes were fighting in the dark' (DP, pp. 35–6).

Nevertheless, for all that it is not consistently developed, the distinction between parties and classes plays a further important role in Kautsky's argument against Lenin. It allows him to erect a clear distinction between the dictatorship of the proletariat on the one hand and the dictatorship of a party on the other. The former refers to the state of affairs in a democracy when the working class eventually gains power, 'a condition which necessarily arises in a real democracy, because of the overwhelming numbers of the proletariat' (ibid., p. 45) – and it is in this connection that Kautsky, like Bernstein, refers to the lessons of the Commune. Since classes rule but do not govern, the dictatorship of a *class* cannot be equated with the dominance of a particular *party*. Thus, as a form of government, dictatorship is no longer that of the proletariat 'but of a proletarian party' (ibid). And where there are several proletarian parties the 'dicatorship of one of these parties is no longer in any sense the dictatorship of the proletariat, but a dictatorship of one part of the proletariat over the other' (ibid., p. 46).

It follows, in Kautsky's view, that there can be no reason to interfere with democracy when the proletariat is in the majority. Thus dictatorship only appears to be necessary when the proletariat is in a minority. Kautsky tries to show that the seizure of power by a minority is a disaster from the point of view of socialism, but his argument on this point does not concern us here. In any case, he claims, such a seizure is premature and unnecessary, for the development of capitalism will itself ensure a substantial working-class majority and the conditions for a democratic transition to socialism.

The main lines of Lenin's response to Kautsky's arguments are well known. Lenin argues that Kautsky grotesquely misrepresents the

sequence of events relating to the congress of soviets and the dissolution
of the democratic assembly, and that he also distorts the conditions under
which sections of the population were excluded from the franchise
covering elections to the soviets. It is not that aspect of Lenin's argument
that concerns us here but rather his analysis of parliamentary
democracy, first his argument that popular, or soviet, democracy
represents a higher form of democracy than the parliamentary assembly,
and second, his analysis of the parliamentary democratic state as a form
of class dictatorship.

On the question of dictatorship and parliamentary democracy Lenin
accuses Kautsky of arguing like a liberal rather than a Marxist by
treating democracy as a non-class issue. Here Lenin follows the
argument of *The State and Revolution* that the state is primarily a
machine for the suppression of one class by another:

never forget that the state even in the most democratic republic, and not only in a
monarchy, is simply a machine for the suppression of one class by another (CW,
vol. 28, p. 369).

This means that every state is a form of class dictatorship and that
Kautsky's counterposition of democracy on the one hand to dictatorship
on the other is based on a fundamental error. A democratic state is a
dictatorship and its democracy is always democracy for one class and
against another. It follows that the form of democracy must change as
one ruling class replaces another. The parliamentary form of state
represents the rule of capital and, in fact, so Lenin argues in his speech
entitled 'The State', 'the more democratic it is the cruder and more
cynical is the rule of capitalism' (CW, vol. 29, p. 485).

How is the class character of parliamentary democracy assured?
First, and most important, the state machinery is not neutral with regard
to the class struggle. The real business of the state goes on, not in the
representative assembly, but in the state apparatuses where the military,
police and civilian bureaucracies function as a more or less unitary body
in the interests of the ruling class. Here state power is conceived both as
representing the interests of a class and as residing in particular state
apparatuses and institutions. State apparatuses are the locus, the means
of action, of state power and, far from acting as instruments of the will of
the assembly, and through that, of the electorate, they act in the interests
of the ruling class. It is precisely because state apparatuses are conceived

in this way, as specific means of action of the power of a class, that they are also conceived as a primary focus of revolutionary action. To capture state power it is necessary to disrupt their unity, set one section of the state power off against another, and to immobilize particular organs of the state. Once captured, a new form of state must be constructed. The old state machine must be smashed and replaced by a state machine of a new type.

It is in this context that Lenin refers to Marx's and Engels's comments on the lessons of the Commune, namely, that 'the working class cannot simply lay hold of the ready-made state machinery and wield it for its own purposes' (MESW, p. 285). Lenin's understanding of these lessons is in marked contrast to that of both Bernstein and Kautsky. For them, the primary lesson of the Commune is that democracy is an indispensable prerequisite for socialism; and in their usage that amounts to an argument for parliamentary democracy. The Parisian working class could not simply lay hold of the existing French state machine because it was not democratic: they therefore set about constructing a democratic state machine of their own. Lenin counters that interpretation with the argument that there is democracy and democracy. Where Kautsky or Bernstein talk of democracy in general they fail to distinguish between bourgeois or parliamentary democracy and popular or soviet de-mocracy. The lesson of the Commune is not that the working class needs democracy in general but that it needs popular democracy in particular.

The class character of democracy is also thought to be assured in two further ways. First, in capitalist societies the democratic rights of freedom of association, press, assembly, etc., in fact benefit the bourgeoisie through its ownership of the media, control over meeting places, money, and other resources. Second, the protection of the rights of individuals and political minorities in bourgeois democracies is a myth. Such recognition or protection is always partial and selective, favouring bourgeois parties, while on all fundamental issues the proletariat 'gets martial law or pogroms, instead of the "protection of the minority"' (CW, vol. 28, p. 245).

Now, we have seen that Kautsky makes precisely these two points in his polemic against Bernstein, and that he uses them to argue the need for working class supremacy in the state. The political significance of money and property and the political partiality of state action are not in dispute between Lenin and Kautsky. What is disputed is the potential power parliamentary democracy gives to a sufficiently strong and determined popular majority – the capacity, in Kautsky's view, of parliament with the backing of the organized working class to push through the socialist transformation of society. It is not the character, the past and present practices of parliamentary regimes that is at issue here but rather their potential for what can be achieved within them. Many of the arguments that Lenin advances against Kautsky have little or no bearing on that point. What is central to Lenin's position is the claim that the very organizational form of the parliamentary democratic state is essentially inimical to the interests of the working class. Those interests can be served only by smashing that form of state and replacing it with something essentially different. One essence must be replaced by another.

Thus, to talk of a democratic and peaceful road to socialism using the procedures of parliamentary democracy is to confuse the issue. Even the most democratic form of state is a class dictatorship – and without class dictatorship there cannot be democracy for that class. Lenin argues that the extent of the franchise does not affect the dictatorial character of the state one way or another. What is crucial rather is the institutional forms within which the franchise operates. For this reason, he claims, the withdrawal of the franchise from the old ruling class and their allies after the revolution 'is not absolutely necessary for the exercise of the dictatorship, it is not an indispensable characteristic of the logical concept of dictatorship' (CW, vol. 28, p. 256).

The essentialism of Lenin's analysis of democratic forms is central to his counterposition of popular, or soviet, democracy on the one hand to parliamentary, or bourgeois, democracy on the other, and to his resolute hostility to any proposal to combine the two. This comes out most clearly in his 'Theses and Report on Bourgeois Democracy and the Dictatorship of the Proletariat', prepared for the First Congress of the Communist International in March 1919:

That proposal indicates the complete ideological bankruptcy of the theorists who defended democracy and failed to see its bourgeois character. This ludicrous attempt to combine the soviet system, i.e., proletarian dictatorship, with the National Assembly, i.e., bourgeois dictatorship, utterly exposes the paucity of thought of the yellow socialists and Social-Democrats, their reactionary petty-bourgeois political outlook, and their cowardly concessions to the irresistibly growing strength of the new, proletarian democracy (CW, vol. 28, p. 467).

The optimism of this last phrase is, to say the least, more than a little premature. But, leaving that aside for the moment, the all-or-nothing character of Lenin's argument is the hallmark of its essentialism. Where parliamentary democracy keeps the mass of the working people far away from the machinery of government, proletarian democracy brings them close to it. Where parliamentary democracy depends on a division of labour between legislature and executive power, proletarian democracy replaces both by 'a self-governing, mass workers' organization' (ibid., p. 459). Where parliamentary democracy elects representatives once every several years, proletarian democracy can recall them on demand. And so it goes on.

Only the soviet organisation of the state can really effect the immediate break-up and total destruction of the old, i.e., bourgeois, bureaucratic and judicial machinery . . . which is the greatest obstacle to the practical implementation of democracy for the workers and working people generally (ibid., p. 466).

For Lenin, the crucial point about the Commune is that it was not a parliamentary institution.

Now, whatever the lessons of the Commune may be, one lesson of the Soviet experience is that the implementation of a popular democratic organization of the state is far easier said than done. The practical, political and organizational, problems of bringing the masses close to the machinery of government, of replacing the state bureaucracies by the 'mass-scale organization' of the working people, are immense, especially where popular organs of struggle have not already been developed in the many areas of state activity that are to be taken over. These problems must be compounded if parliamentary forms of representation and control over state apparatuses are rejected out of hand. That, of course, is precisely the issue raised by Kautsky's argument that 'control of government is the most important duty of parliament, and in this it can be replaced by no other institution' (DP, p. 26). However limited the effectiveness of parliamentary control may be, there is a point to Kautsky's argument that is evaded in Lenin's essentialist rejection of parliamentary institutions as a form of bourgeois dictatorship. It is all very well to talk of dispensing with parliamentary-bureaucratic forms of state organization when some alternative forms of popular control and self-organization have been developed. Otherwise, it amounts to proposing that we dismantle even the limited form of popular control over the bureaucratic state machinery that parliament represents.

III. PROBLEMS IN THE MARXIST THEORY OF POLITICS AND THE STATE

The disputes over the relationship between classes and their interests on the one hand and the institutional conditions and features of parliamentary democracy on the other take us to the heart of the most fundamental problems of Marxist analyses of politics, and they raise some particular problems concerning the analysis of politics in parliamentary regimes. We have seen that Kautsky repudiates Bernstein's characterization of democracy as the abolition of class government, if not yet the absence of classes, and that Lenin accuses Kautsky of ignoring the class character of democracy. It is important to be clear about the nature of these differences. At first glance the points at issue seem straightforward enough, and it would be all too easy to play Lenin, Kautsky and Bernstein off against each other: to note the essentialism of Lenin's account of parliamentary democracy and to argue, with Kautsky, that the class character of the parliamentary state is not an all-or-nothing affair, that it could be utterly transformed by a parliamentary majority with the backing of a sufficiently-determined popular majority outside parliament; or to argue, on the other hand, that Bernstein's account of democratic government, of its non-class character and its protection of minorities, ignores the entrenched position of capital in modern democratic societies and the fact that minorities are often given a very rough time in them. It would be all too easy, in other words, to present Kautsky as a reasoned exponent of the democratic road to socialism, avoiding the polar extremes of Lenin's essentialism and of Bernstein's revisionism. This may seem all the more tempting at a time when the diverse strands of 'Eurocommunism' are insisting on the necessity of a democratic road and have begun to distance themselves from the 'Leninist' theory of politics and the state.

Such an account would not survive close inspection – and nor would the rather different accounts required to erect Bernstein or Lenin as the hero. It is true that Kautsky avoids the economism of Lenin, but he does so only by erecting an economism of his own: we have noted his confusions and sleight of hand over the relations between classes and parties and his reliance on the economic tendencies of capitalist development to furnish an organized political majority for socialism. Or again, we have seen that there is little to choose between Kautsky and Bernstein over the power that parliamentary government gives to a sufficiently determined popular majority. The point of Bernstein's account of democracy as the suppression of class government is not to deny that the bourgeoisie may be well entrenched but rather to insist that that is not built in to the structure of democratic politics.

The trouble with the game of playing these positions off against each other, or for that matter against the diverse writings of Marx or Engels or Gramsci, is that it fails to consider what it is about Marxist analyses of politics and the state that makes such disputes possible and so difficult to resolve. In Marxist discourse problems of political analysis are posed in relation to a conception of society as essentially structured by the economy and, in particular, by the distribution of the population into classes with distinct and ultimately incompatible interests. Politics is then conceived as a sphere of representation of those interests and a crucial site of the struggle between them. This notion of representation is central: it means that classes and their interests are distinct from political organizations, state apparatuses and ideologies and yet are represented by them; that politics is fundamentally determined by the economy, by classes and their interests on the one hand, yet not fully determined on the other. It means, in other words, that there are features of political life not fully determined by classes and their interests. This is the point of the slogans of determination by the economy in the last instance (but not before), relative autonomy, and the like. They try both to open a conceptual space for non-economic, non-class determinants of political life and to stop it getting out of hand.

Now, there is one crucial respect in which what is at issue between Lenin and Kautsky or Kautsky and Bernstein is the question not so much of the existence of this conceptual space but rather of the precise location of its boundaries, and in that respect their arguments are little more than variations on a single theme. Consider first the Lenin–Kautsky debate. Politics, for Kautsky, is class struggle. The working class struggles first to obtain democracy and then to use it to effect the transfer of state power and the socialist transformation of society. Here democracy is more than a matter of universal suffrage since it also requires that the state apparatuses are subject to parliamentary control. And the strength of parliament depends on the balance between the classes backing it and those opposed to it. But, given the suffrage, the tendencies of capitalist development and the experiences of class struggle will ensure in the long run a parliamentary majority for socialism backed by a sufficiently strong and organized working class. Thus Kautsky presents democracy, first, as the product of popular struggle, second, as ensuring the victory of socialism, and third as providing institutional conditions in which state power may be held by either the bourgeoisie or the proletariat. These institutional conditions can be conceived therefore both as representing the long-term interests of a class and as providing a neutral arena in which the classes contend for power.

However, it is this last point which leads Lenin to accuse Kautsky of arguing like a liberal rather than a Marxist. Lenin maintains, as we have seen, that the institutional conditions of parliamentary democracy provide an arena of struggle that is in no sense neutral as between the contending classes. Parliamentary democracy with its periodic elections and division of labour between legislature and executive reflects the interests of the bourgeoisie. It must be overthrown and replaced by a proletarian democracy, the institutional reflection of the interests of the working class and working people generally. From this perspective it is clear that to argue, as Kautsky does, that state power in a democracy may be held by the bourgeoisie or by the proletariat is to ignore essential class determinants of the institutional forms of political life. But, if the state and the institutional forms of politics essentially reflect the interests of a class, there is a sense in which political practices are not always so determined. To take an example that is especially pertinent in the present context, Lenin maintains that the practices of social democracy may, and sometimes do, fundamentally betray the interests of the working class. Those practices are determined, not directly by these interests but rather by struggle: in this case by the struggle between Marxism and the varieties of revisionism, reformism and other tendencies that beset it. However much some of these tendencies may themselves be thought to represent the interests of classes, and Lenin clearly allows of other 'interests', e.g. of 'nationalities', the practices of social democracy are determined not directly by the interests themselves but by the struggle between them, or rather between their representatives. Thus, although he draws the boundaries in a different place than Kautsky, Lenin's argument too requires a conceptual space for crucial features of politics that are not simply class determined.

We can now quickly consider Kautsky and Bernstein. In one sense, as I have suggested, there is little to choose between their analyses of the potentialities of parliamentary democracy. But Bernstein conceives of democracy as the absence of class government, a conception to which Kautsky is resolutely opposed. What is at issue between them seems to be the connection between classes and the forces engaged in political struggle. For Kautsky, those forces are classes or the representatives of classes – and we have seen some of the confusions this leads him into. Bernstein's position is less clear cut. Although he continues to refer to classes and their interests, and to the working class as a political force, it seems clear that he regards the movement towards socialism as not primarily a *class* issue at all. We have seen how Bernstein rejects the view that the tendencies of capitalist development can be relied on to produce a proletarian majority whose experience of struggle would weld them into an overwhelming force for socialism. Thus, if a political majority for socialism is to be achieved it cannot be constructed simply out of the interests of the working class. It must rather be constructed through argument and persuasion, through the construction of alliances, till it embraces people of good will from all sections of the population. This is the point of Bernstein's conception of democracy: it means not the suppression of government by one class and its replacement by another but the end of class government as such. Instead government will be by political majorities constructed around programmes and objectives, and hopefully around the ethical ideal of socialism, not around the interests of classes. In this sense the forces engaged in democratic politics need not be restricted to classes and their representatives. But, the role ascribed here to ethical ideals is itself conceived as being a function of economic development:

Modern society is much richer than earlier societies in ideologies which are not determined by economics and by nature working as an economic force . . . in order to leave no room for misconception, the point of economic development attained today leaves the ideological, and especially the ethical factors greater space for independent activity than was formerly the case (ES, p. 15).

Here, non-class, non-economic determinants of social life are invoked but they are confined within bounds given by the development of the economy. For all his revisionism and his reassertion of an ethical basis for socialism, Bernstein does not completely break with the Marxist conception of the ultimately determining role of the economy. What must be noted for our purposes is that his discussion extends the space for significant non-class, non-economic determinants of political life beyond the bounds set by Kautsky.

But, to return to the question of what it is about Marxism that makes these differences at once possible and so difficult to resolve, there is a sense in which what is at issue between Kautsky, Bernstein and Lenin is a matter of variations on the single crucial theme of representation, determination in the last instance, relative autonomy, and the like. It is a matter of conceiving a relationship between the economy and politics, between the distribution of the population into classes on the one hand and political organizations, institutions and ideologies on the other, that is able to combine the ultimately determining role of the economy with the irreducibility of political life. Such a relationship must open a conceptual space for effective non-class, non-economic features of political life and keep them closely circumscribed: political life must be autonomous, but only relatively so. What is at issue, then, is not the existence of such a conceptual space but rather the way it is conceived and the precise location of its boundaries.

What makes these differences possible within Marxism is simply that, for all the wealth of assertions that the economy assumes the fundamental role, but only in the last instance, and for all the diverse formulations of that idea, the precise mechanisms of the supposed relationship between economic 'base' and political 'superstructure' are nowhere clearly specified. 'Determination in the last instance' and all the other slogans are little more than a gesture towards a theoretical vacancy that always remains to be filled. It is because they are little more than a gesture that Lenin, Kautsky and Bernstein, and subsequently any number of others, can erect their different conceptions of the elements of political life that are or are not directly tied to class or economic determinations.

However, and this brings us to the fundamental problem, it is not merely that this theoretical vacancy is left open. The problem is that it cannot be filled: the slogans of 'relative autonomy', 'determination in the last instance', and all the rest, are gestural evasions of a problem that cannot be resolved. There is no coherent way in which political life can be conceived as different from and irreducible to the economy and the distribution of the population into classes on the one hand and in which the economy is conceived as playing the ultimately determining role on the other. In this respect the positions of Lenin, Kautsky and Bernstein are predicated on somewhat different evasions of the same fundamental problem; and that is why there can be no resolution of the differences between them. That there can be no coherent conception of 'determination in the last instance' and 'relative autonomy' has been argued by me and my co-authors in *Marx's* Capital *and Capitalism Today*. There is no need to repeat that argument here and it will be sufficient merely to indicate the nature of the problem: any such conception must allow for elements of political life that are both effective and irreducible on the one hand and yet constrain their effectiveness to conform to the supposed ultimately determining role of the economic on the other. Now, it may be suggested that there are conceptions of relative autonomy that do not involve this difficulty. Indeed, some of our critics have made that suggestion, but none has come out with a developed concept of relative autonomy that does the trick. Let me just say that the time is past when Marxists could get by with the assertion of relative autonomy, that the onus is on advocates of this and other related concepts to establish the mechanism of the supposed ultimately determining role of the economy, to show how they are effective rather than merely assert that they are.

To say that there can be no coherent conception of 'relative autonomy' is to say that the question of a relationship between political life and the economy that is able to combine the ultimately determining role of the one with the irreducibility of the other is wrongly posed, that we need to address a different set of questions. It is not to say that there are no connections between the diverse struggles to be found in modern society and the structure of its economy. Nor is it to say that politics is *absolutely* autonomous – whatever that may be thought to mean. It is to say that whatever connections there may be, there is no one general mechanism of connection between politics and the economy that is characteristic of capitalism as such – or, for that matter, of particular historical phases of its development. This is not, of course, to deny that conceptions of the interests of a class, and organizations claiming to represent such interest, may sometimes play a significant political role, or that certain business or financial interests may be well entrenched in the dominant forms of politics and the state. The point rather is that where such organizations or entrenched interests exist and are effective, it is as the outcome of struggle, perhaps of a series of struggles, to mobilize support around specific objectives, to defeat opposing attempts at mobilization, to establish particular organizational forms (in Labour Party, in the structure of the NHS, or other state apparatuses) and so on – not of any necessities that may be thought to arise out of the character of capitalist economic relations.

Where does all this leave us with regard to parliamentary democracy? We are concerned with the forms and conditions of struggle in societies with parliamentary democratic forms of government, and with the options for a socialist politics under those conditions. I have argued that political analysis conducted in terms of an imagery of economic determination and struggle between classes must be fundamentally inadequate, whether the imagery be that of Lenin or Kautsky or one of the numerous others available in contemporary Marxism. The problem is not to establish the class character of democracy, to identify the class character of political forces, to construct alliances between classes and other interests, or whatever. It is to mobilize effective support around socialist objectives out of the forces, struggles and ideologies operative in particular societies. But to do that, we need to develop our analysis of parliamentary conditions of struggle. And this brings us back to another aspect of the Lenin, Kautsky, Bernstein debates for, although there is a crucial respect in which the differences between them amount to different evasions of an insoluble problem, what they have to say about parliamentary democracy is by no means reducible to these evasions. It is to this other aspect of their arguments that we now turn.

IV. THE ANALYSIS OF POLITICS IN PARLIAMENTARY DEMOCRATIC REGIMES

If we abstract from the imagery of class and economic determination which characterizes so much of the debate between them, there remain important issues to be considered in relation first to Lenin's counterposition of parliamentary and popular democracy and, second, to the analysis of parliamentary democracy itself.

On the first set of issues, it is clear that although Lenin represents the counterposition as one between bourgeois and proletarian democracy his characterizations are not exhausted in that representation. To discuss these issues at length would take us beyond the scope of the present paper, and I shall concentrate here on parliamentary democracy. But it may be worth noting a couple of points on what Lenin presents as the polar alternative. The first point is that, although they have no truck with Lenin's essentialist counterposition, both Kautsky and Bernstein identify socialism with the development of what Bernstein calls 'an elaborately organized self-government' (ES, p. 155). There is no dispute over the conception of socialism as being fundamentally democratic, and over the consequent need to go beyond the limits of parliamentary democratic forms. Unfortunately, and this is the second point, what is involved in going beyond those limits remains remarkably unclear and, in Lenin's case, dangerously so.

It would not be too unfair to say that Marxist discussions of popular democracy have barely advanced beyond Rousseau. What would the government of society as 'a self-governing, mass workers' organization' look like in, say, Lenin's Russia or in Britain today? As for the notion of 'recall on demand', proposed as an alternative to institutionalized and periodic elections, it is clearly unworkable for all but the most minute constituencies. Otherwise, it is in danger of being merely utopian. In a constituency of, say, 50,000 persons the notion of 'recall on demand' has no determinate meaning, except in terms of particular institutionalized forms of making that demand manifest. Suppose for example, that the voting machinery may be set in motion on receipt of the signatures of not less than a hundred, or not less that a thousand electors, then the effects of such a system of 'recall on demand' would depend on the minimum figure chosen. The alternative to a system of institutionalized direct elections is not the absence of institutionalization but some other institutionalized system: either a different system of direct election or a system of numerous minute constituencies such that the membership of central decision-making bodies is effectively chosen by some indirect, but equally institutionalized, procedure. Whatever the merits of different systems may be, it cannot be argued that parliamentary elections erect a division between the people and their representatives which 'recall on demand' is able to overcome.

These and other such slogans gloss over the considerable problems of integration and coordination of numerous distinct and internally complex political and economic practices – which would be the more acute if both parliamentary-bureaucratic and commodity forms of organization and distribution were to be excluded. I raise this point not in order to deny the possibility of popular-democratic forms of organization but rather, as I have already suggested, to indicate the dangers of any all-or-nothing opposition and the scale of the problems that have yet to be resolved. We have to develop both our conceptions of what the democratization of significant areas of social life would involve and the organizational forms in which we could begin to realize it.

Turning to the analysis of parliamentary democracy, we have seen that both Bernstein and Kautsky, in rather different forms, regard parliamentary democracy as a means whereby the government of society may be taken into the hands of a popular majority, arguing that a popular majority can be translated into a parliamentary majority and that a parliamentary majority, backed by a determined popular majority, can subject the state machinery to its will. Leaving aside the question of the supposed class character of democracy, Lenin attacks this position on two levels by arguing first that the 'real business' of the state goes on in the bureaucracy rather than in parliament, and secondly that in capitalist society the conditions of electoral struggle are fundamentally distorted by money and property, control of the media and of meeting places, and so on.

It is important to be clear what is at issue here. The arguments of Kautsky and Bernstein reproduce many of the crucial features of a constitutional mode of discourse, that is, of a mode of discourse that is concerned to attribute sovereignty to the state and to a specific location within it, so that other elements of the state may be conceived as agencies of the sovereign power. In effect, the argument is that parliament is, or may be, both sovereign and representative of the popular will. Lenin's response is not so much to question the pertinence of that mode of discourse but rather first to question the location of sovereign power and its representative character (it does not reside in parliament but in the bureaucracy and it represents the bourgeoisie not the popular will), and second, to question the representative nature of parliament and electoral struggle.

This is not the place for a discussion of constitutional discourse and the theory of sovereignty, but it is important to register its effects with regard to the conception of the state as a unitary agency whose actions express the sovereign will. Rather than take the unity of the state as given, we are concerned to analyse it as a specific set of institutions and arenas of struggle subject to definite internal connections and relations to other agencies and forces – and there are significant contexts in which Lenin does analyse the state in such terms. As for constitutional discourse, the point is not to deny its importance but rather to locate its significance in the way it is, or may be, deployed in particular political arenas.

There are many serious and difficult issues to be considered here and I shall restrict myself to indicating some of the problems that must be confronted in any serious investigation of the character of parliamentary democratic conditions of struggle. Some of these problems have received an extensive, if not very satisfactory, discussion in the non-Marxist, academic literature, but I shall not attempt to deal with that literature here.

(i) Parliament and state apparatuses

Lenin's position is clear: parliament is a talking shop and the real business of the state goes on behind the scenes. It is on this point, amongst others, that he accuses Kautsky of arguing like a liberal rather than a Marxist. The accusation is unfair, for Kautsky's point is not that parliament does control the state apparatuses but that it can be made into a means of doing so: in the last resort the power of parliament depends 'on the energy and courage of the classes behind it and on the energy and courage of the classes on which its will is to be imposed' (CS, p. 187). Thus, for Kautsky, the growing strength and political maturity of the working class will eventually lead to the dominant position of parliament within the state. Abstracting from his confusion over classes and political forces, the argument is that the power of parliament within the state depends on the strength of the forces backing it as against those which favour other means of effecting state action.

Kautsky's argument has the merit of avoiding the worst effects of Lenin's essentialism since it assigns no essential character to the relations between parliament and state apparatuses and treats them rather as subject to variation and struggle. Unfortunately he gives no account of the mechanisms whereby parliamentary control is to be made effective or of the role of popular struggle in securing them. Kautsky's argument that parliament can exercise effective control, and Lenin's reply that it cannot, both concern the attribution of sovereignty, and they pay no further attention to the question of what the connections are between parliament and other state apparatuses or of how they should be analysed.

What is at issue here is not just a question of political analysis, of identifying arenas of struggle and the forces engaged in them. It is also a question of democratic theory. We are concerned with the democratization not of a sovereign power but rather of particular significant spheres of social organization. In that sense whether a system of government is to be regarded as democratic or not must surely depend not only on the character of its electoral arrangements but also on the effective relations between the elected assembly (or assembly plus president) and the practices of the state apparatuses. I stress *effective* relations here since, once the question of sovereignty has been displaced, it is clear that what those relations are is not determined by their representation in constitutional discourse. In the case of Britain, for example, it is well known that for all the talk of the sovereignty of parliament there are significant constraints on parliamentary control of the state apparatuses and even of the cabinet. A society may be democratic as far as its electoral machinery and constitutional law are concerned and extremely undemocratic with regard to control over the practices of the state.

Of course Lenin and Kautsky are not alone in leaving this gap in their analyses of parliamentary democracy, and it can certainly be found in much non-Marxist democratic theory. But, to pose the problem of the connections between parliament and the state apparatuses is also to problematize the senses in which state apparatuses may be or should be subjected to parliamentary control. Notice, first, that it is too simplistic to examine these connections in terms of control or the absence of control. The radical democratic critique of parliamentary democracy has always insisted that the bureaucratic mode of government is itself a creature of the parliamentary separation of legislature from executive. This point can be found in Marx's commentary on the Paris Commune and in much of Lenin's writings on the state. The very separation between parliament, a body which issues decrees, laws and instructions, and bodies which are supposed to put them into effect both poses the problem of parliamentary control and imposes limits to its effectiveness. Consider the means of control actually or potentially available to parliament: issue of laws, decrees and instructions, questioning of ministers and civil servants, parliamentary committees of inquiry and investigative subcommittees, and so on. Simply to list the possible instruments of control is to recognize their limitations, to note the correlative opportunities for evasion and misdirection and the fact that no parliamentary body can hope to investigate more than a small part of the activities of the state. Contrary to Kautsky's attribution of a potential sovereign power to parliament, there are inescapable limits to the power of parliament within the state.

It would be absurd to pretend that any existing parliamentary assembly has even approached the limits of control that are in principle open to it. But what those inescapable limits show is that state apparatuses can never be reduced to the mere instruments of parliament's intentions. And to say that is to open up a field of investigation that has been unduly neglected by Marxist analysis of the state. To say that they cannot be mere instruments is to say that state apparatuses must be considered as, or as containing, political forces in their own right, subject indeed to constraints in the form of cabinet or parliamentary 'controls', but nevertheless with complex internal structures and relations with other state apparatuses and political forces generally. It is to say that state apparatuses or sections within them may themselves act on the conditions of struggle in parliament, cabinet and the electorate; that they may be subject to constraints and influences of various kinds from other state apparatuses and from forces outside parliament; that the effects of their actions cannot be reduced to the statutes they are supposed to enforce and instructions they are supposed to implement.

If we are concerned with the problems of extending democratic control in Britain then we must also be concerned to investigate the forms of organization of the various state apparatuses and their connections with each other, with parliament and with cabinet, the means of control presently employed and how they can be extended and, last but not least, the relations that exist between state apparatuses on the one hand and extra-parliamentary political forces on the other. What these relationships and connections are, and their political significance, cannot be deduced from the mere fact of parliamentary government. We must beware of easy generalizations about what may or may not be possible in Britain or anywhere else merely because there are democratic forms of government.

Finally, that there are inescapable limits to the power of parliament within the state means also that we should be concerned to develop other forms of democratic supervision and control over the state apparatuses involving, for example, wider public access to information, investigative journalism and forms of popular intervention in the functioning of particular state apparatuses. The point here is not to accept either Lenin's counterposition of parliamentary and popular democracy or, for that matter, Kautsky's counterposition of control by a central assembly to control by 'an unorganized and formless mass of people', as if those were the only alternatives. The extension of democracy requires that organs of popular control be developed, not that parliament be overthrown.

(ii) Parliament and people

We can now turn to the relations between parliament and the electorate and the conditions of electoral struggle. We have seen that Bernstein regards the right to vote as being, in the long run, 'the implement by which to transform the representatives of the people from masters into real servants of the people' (ES, p. 144). If we are to take seriously that conception of representatives as, potentially, 'real servants of the people' we must suppose that the activities of parties reflect the desires of 'the people' but play no part in the formation of those desires. To the extent that parties are conceived as representing popular concerns they cannot also be conceived as determinants of what they represent. In Bernstein's argument the machinery of parliamentary elections appears simply as a means of aggregating the interests or wishes of an underlying population: different sections of the population may have different interests and/or wishes and these are brought together in elections and reflected in the relative strengths of parties and groups in parliament.

Kautsky has a different view of parliamentary democracy, but it is still seen as involving the subordination of government to a popular majority. The character of parliament reflects the extent of the franchise, and parties represent classes, so that their electoral support is a measure of the strength of the classes represented. The experience of economic and political struggle will lead the working class to the recognition that its interests are irrevocably opposed to those of the bourgeoisie, while the tendencies of capitalist economic development will ensure a working-class majority. Thus, in the long run, the numerical strength of the working class will be reflected in a parliamentary majority for socialism. Here too the electoral machinery is conceived as a means of aggregating popular concerns. While the activities of parties may have an impact on what those concerns are, the underlying tendencies of capitalism ensure in the long run that the expressed concerns of the working class correspond to their real interests.

So, in spite of their differences, Bernstein and Kautsky share a conception of parliamentary democracy as in the long run resulting in a situation where parties and groupings in parliament do represent the interests or desires of an underlying population. But the presumption of that long-run situation involves two further presumptions: first, that the votes of the electorate reflect interests and/or desires that are formed independently of the practices of parties and other agencies, and second, that these are effectively aggregated through elections. Lenin challenges both presumptions. Of course he does not dispute Kautsky's view that there are real or 'objective' class interests not dependent on party practices, but he clearly regards those interests as being fundamentally misrepresented and distorted in bourgeois democracy by the social distribution of money and property, control of the media, and other conditions of electoral struggle. The franchise and electoral machinery are likewise seen as rigged in favour of the bourgeoisie. Lenin also disputes the accountability of members of parliamentary assemblies, arguing instead for a system of recall on demand – and we have seen the utopian dangers involved in that part of his critique.

But the other points at issue in these differences between Lenin, Kautsky and Bernstein raise fundamental problems of the concep- tualization of the field of electoral struggle. We are concerned with an electorate, organized into constituencies, whose votes are aggregated by an electoral machine to produce an outcome in the form of a distribution of seats to parties. How members of the electorate vote depends on a variety of external conditions and complex internal processes. The external conditions include the practices of other agencies, political parties, trades unions, industrial and financial enterprises, churches, media, sections of the state apparatuses, and so on, which do not vote but may nevertheless, as Lenin argues, significantly affect the pattern of voting. Now, what Bernstein and Kautsky represent as the long-run effect of parliamentary democracy requires us to envisage a situation in which the voting intentions of the electors reflect interests or desires that are formed independently of the practices of those other agencies. That idea has only to be clearly stated for its absurdity to become apparent: it requires either a realm of constitutive subjects endowed with free will and an autonomous capacity for rational calculation and decision, the unmoved movers of society and history, or else, as with Kautsky, it requires that the practices of these other agencies do in the long run accord with the class interests that are given in the structure of the economy. Both are reductionist, towards the constitutive actions of individuals on the one hand and the ultimately determining role of the economy on the other.

But to reject these reductionisms is to argue that the practices of parties and other agencies may significantly affect the pattern of voting – and there is no need to argue further, as with Lenin, that the net effect of these other agencies is to represent the interests of the bourgeoisie, thus invoking yet another reductionism. To say that these other agencies may affect the pattern of voting is to say, first, that parties cannot be regarded merely as representing popular concerns, for they can also be significant determinants of those concerns, and to say, more generally, that electoral outcomes cannot be regarded as the product of the interests or desires of the electorate. They are the product of a complex play of forces in which electors themselves are never the only effective actors.

As for the aggregate character of elections it is clear that what is aggregated is *votes*, not the concerns of individual electors, and that electors may cast their votes in a similar way for a variety of different reasons. That point may seem trivial but it has important implications. In particular, it means that the extent to which electoral outcomes reflect the concerns of the electors is not determined by the character of the electoral machinery as such. It depends rather on the character of the voting choices that are put before them, on the issues that are subject to debate within and between the competing parties. In this respect too it is clear that electoral outcomes cannot be regarded as the product of the interests or desires of the electorate. There may well be issues of widespread popular concern that are barely represented in electoral outcomes. The other side of electoral aggregation concerns its effects on the relative strength of the competing parties. It is well known that different ways of aggregating the same set of votes can produce widely different outcomes, that changes in electoral machinery can significantly affect the character of party competition, and there are well-known cases where governing parties have been known to gerrymander constituency boundaries in their favour. But we can register these effects without supposing that they necessarily emanate from the interests of the bourgeoisie.

These arguments too pose problems for political analysis and for our conception of democracy. First, to say that parties compete in an electoral arena is hardly an adequate specification of the character of that arena of the parties and other forces active in it. The problem here is that to describe a form of politics as parliamentary democratic is to say very little about the political forces at work in the society or the sites of struggle and political issues in which they are engaged. Electoral and parliamentary arenas are by no means exclusive of other arenas of struggle or of significant non-electoral agencies acting on the various state apparatuses, parliament, and the electoral arena itself. What those agencies are and the effects they may have can vary considerably over time or from one parliamentary democracy to another, and it is impossible to assume that the electorate and elected assembly necessarily constitute the sole, or even the most, significant arenas of political struggle. It follows that there can be few worthwhile general propositions concerning the political effects of parliamentary democracy or the character of political struggle in democratic societies.

To see the problem this poses for our conception of democracy it is sufficient to note that electoral struggles must always involve the play of diverse forces and agencies, that this is an inescapable feature of democratic politics. We have seen that parliamentary democratic government always presupposes the existence of state apparatuses. Since they must be considered as, or as containing, political actors in their own right, it follows that, even if we leave aside the question of parties and other non-state agencies, there cannot be a parliamentary democracy in which the electorate is not subject to the play of non-voting but nevertheless effective agencies. It is impossible then to argue that the media or other agencies *distort* some presumably underlying set of concerns, for what the concerns of the electorate are must always depend on the actions of some set of forces or other. The distribution of forces may change but it cannot be eliminated. For similar reasons it is impossible to argue that the aggregative effects of particular electoral arrangements *distort* the wishes of the electorate. Different electoral arrangements have different effects, and we may wish to argue that some are preferable to others. But what those effects are will depend on the character of the parties and other forces at work in the electoral arena. They are never simply a product of electoral arrangements as such.

I have already suggested that the democratic character of a system of government must depend on the effective connections between the elected assembly and the practices of the state apparatuses as well as on its electoral arrangements. The present argument poses an issue at the level of those electoral arrangements. The extent to which a society may be regarded as democratic must surely depend not only on the extent to which there is electoral competition between parties – 'pluralism' as it is sometimes called – but also on the character of those parties and the other effective political forces. It is by no means obvious then that a situation of inter-party competition is necessarily more democratic than single party government. And where there is party competition it seems clear, for example, that legal regulation of contributions to political parties or expenditure on election campaigns may significantly reduce the impact of the distribution of wealth on the field of electoral struggle. Or again, we might consider the effects of changes in the organization and control of the media, or of the way they are financed, of the appointment of worker directors to the Boards of large companies, and so on. These examples show that we need to extend our analysis of what is democratic about parliamentary democracy, to develop means of assessing the impact of forces that are active in or upon the electoral field as well as the formal character of electoral arrangements, and means of arguing that the practices of some parties and forces make a society less democratic than it might otherwise be.

CONCLUSIONS

This paper has considered the major arguments of the debates between Bernstein and Kautsky, Kautsky and Lenin concerning parliamentary democracy and socialism. I have argued that some of the differences between them amount to different gestures towards a solution of the same glaring problem, namely, how to combine a conception of the ultimately determining role of the economy, of classes and their interests and the conflicts between them, with acknowledgement of the irreducibility of politics and ideology. Indeed the greater part of Marxist theoretical work on politics and the state consists of diverse and more or less sophisticated stabs at that problem and of interminable disputes between them. My co-authors and I have argued in *Marx's* Capital *and Capitalism Today* that that problem cannot be resolved, so that no proposed 'solution' can ever be more than gestural. There is no *general* mechanism of connection between the economic relations of a society, the relations between classes and whatever objective interests may be ascribed to them, and the formation of arenas of struggle in that society, the organization of forces engaged in them and the issues and ideologies on which they divide.

I am not saying here that there are no connections between the economy and arenas of struggle, still less, as has sometimes been alleged, that politics is absolutely autonomous (whatever that is supposed to mean). But what the connections are may vary and we should not expect the connections that obtain between economic relations and the formation of arenas of struggle and forces engaged in them to conform to any single general model of determination. Unfortunately, the fact that so much Marxist work on politics has been organized in terms of some gestural solution or other to the problem of a single general mechanism has had serious consequences for the way the struggles, the conditions in which they take place, and the forces engaged in them are analysed. Too often, Marxist political analysis has the effect of neglecting the specificity of particular struggles and forces, and of relations between them, by dissolving them into classes, class fractions and their supposed interests, while invoking 'anti-economism' or 'relative autonomy' to soak up any residue.

But, whether or not that argument is accepted, it is clear that the diverse arguments of Lenin, Kautsky and Bernstein do pose serious problems that are not simply a matter of Bernstein's or Kautsky's 'revisionism' or of Lenin's or Kautsky's 'economism'. At this level the disputes are effectively concerned with the location of sovereign power and its representative character. I have argued that once the issue of sovereignty is displaced it becomes possible to pose a number of serious problems with regard to the analysis of politics under conditions of parliamentary democracy and also in relation to our conceptions of democracy and democratization.

These problems have been discussed first in relation to the connections between parliament and the various state apparatuses, and I have argued that parliamentary government both presupposes bureaucratic state apparatuses and poses the problem of their control; that there are unavoidable limits to the capacities of parliaments to control their state apparatuses; and that state apparatuses or sections within them may be significant political forces in their own right, acting subject to constraints imposed by their relation to parliament, cabinet and other state apparatuses on the one hand, and their relation to various non-state political forces on the other. But none of those points requires that we conceive the parliamentary state as necessarily furthering the interests of particular classes or as posing insuperable obstacles to a peaceful and democratic process of socialization. Because of the limits to parliamentary control over the state apparatuses I have argued that the democratization of our society requires the development of extra-parliamentary forms of supervision and control in particular spheres of state activity.

Second, in relation to the field of electoral struggle, I have argued that parliament and the electoral process cannot be analysed as aggregating the concerns of the electorate; that those concerns are in part dependent on the practices of parties and other political forces so that they cannot be conceived as independent determinants of those practices; that the extent to which popular concerns are reflected in electoral outcomes is a function not so much of the strength of those concerns but rather of the issues in debate between and within parties; that the conditions of electoral struggle may have differential effects on competing political positions; and finally, that the democratic character of an electoral system should be assessed not only in relation to the question of electoral competition between parties but also in relation to the characters of the parties themselves and of other forces acting on the field of electoral struggle. These points, too, can be made without supposing an essential bias in favour of the bourgeoisie and against socialism.

In both cases the major problems for political analysis concern the identification of arenas of struggle, of the forces engaged and the issues at stake in them. To describe a society as parliamentary democratic is to say very little about what those arenas, forces and issues are, or about what forms of struggle are either possible or desirable. These must be matters for detailed analysis of the society in question, not for vague propositions about parliamentary democracy in general. There may well be significant obstacles to socialist politics in many parliamentary democracies, but that is always a matter of particular political conditions (some of which may be extremely difficult to overcome) rather than a property of parliamentary democracy as such. Above all, it is important to beware of the twin illusions of parliamentarism: to imagine, because parliamentary democracy involves competition for power between parties, on the one hand that there are not other significant political forces acting on the state apparatuses, the electorate and parliament itself, and on the other that parties and the electoral struggles between them are the only significant arenas of political struggle.

REFERENCES

Bernstein, Eduard, *Evolutionary Socialism*, Schocken Books, New York, 1961.
Cutler, Antony, Hindess, Barry, Hirst, Paul, Hussain, Athar, *Marx's* Capital *and Capitalism Today*, Routledge & Kegan Paul, London, 1977.
Kautsky, Karl, *The Class Struggle*, W. W. Norton & Co., New York, 1971.
Kautsky, Karl, *The Dictatorship of the Proletariat*, University of Michigan Press, Ann Arbor, 1964.
Kautsky, Karl, *Bernstein und das sozialdemokratische Programm. Eine Antikritik*, Stuttgart, 1899.
Lenin, V. I., *The State and Revolution* in *Collected Works*, vol. 25, Lawrence & Wishart, London, 1964.
Lenin, V. I., 'The Proletarian Revolution and the Renegade Kautsky', and 'Theses and Report on Bourgeois Democracy and the Dictatorship of the Proletariat', both in *Collected Works*, vol. 28, Lawrence & Wishart, London, 1964.
Marx, Karl, and Engels, Frederick, *Selected Works in One Volume*, Lawrence & Wishart, London, 1970.

THE POLITICAL INDETERMINACY
OF DEMOCRACY*

Bob Jessop

It is a frequently-remarked paradox that democratic institutions should exist in class societies since majority rule seems inconsistent with minority exploitation. But there is less agreement about the implications of this paradox. For it is uncertain whether it justifies the conclusion that the bourgeois democratic republic is the best possible political shell for capitalism or that capitalism is a necessary condition for the full realization of democracy. Conversely one might question whether democracy permits the tendential elimination of capitalist exploitation and/or if such exploitation is incompatible with the effective functioning of democratic institutions. It is such problems that concern us in this paper. However, rather than confront them immediately and directly, we intend to examine them through the development of a theory of 'pure democracy'. This analysis is then linked to the nature of the state and class struggle in bourgeois societies. In this way it is hoped to draw out certain conclusions about the contradictions of capitalist democracy that might otherwise remain unstated.

POPULAR DEMOCRACY AND CLASS DICTATORSHIP

In general terms 'democracy' refers to 'government by the people'. This definition immediately raises three issues: the nature of government, the nature of the people, and the nature of the relation between government and people. In particular it is important to establish the relation between these concepts and those traditionally emphasized in Marxist political

* Although it has been revised and expanded since it was originally delivered in December 1978, this paper still contains a number of provisional and/or hesitant arguments concerning democracy and 'people formation'. Accordingly, while I would like to record the influence of Ernesto Laclau and Adam Przeworski on certain formulations, it is particularly important to emphasize that I alone am responsible for the present arguments and their conclusions.

theories, that is, 'state', 'class', and 'dictatorship'. It is only through a confrontation of these concepts that we can clarify the connection between 'government by the people' and 'the rule of capital'. Let us begin with those of 'government' and 'state'.

These concepts both refer to a 'public power' which emerges at a certain stage in the development of the division of labour and undertakes certain essential functions in its coordination. This power is liable to two kinds of transformation. On the one hand it can change through the concentration of public functions in a system of specialized political apparatuses with permanent staff, thereby producing an institutional separation of 'state' and 'society' and a possible contradiction between 'officialdom' and 'people'. On the other hand it can be changed through the consolidation of relations of production based on the appropriation by one class of surplus-labour performed by another: the public power is thereby overdetermined in its structure and operation by class relations and practices and thus expresses the contradiction between the exploiting and exploited classes. This means the state is situated at the intersection of two sets of relations and must be considered in terms of the interaction between them.

It should be emphasized that the 'officialdom-people' and the 'class-class' determinations are analytically distinct and that each reveals certain conditions of existence and/or effects which are more or less independent of those involved in the other. It should also be noted that the relative weight of these determinations can vary so that, in Mao's terms, either could become the basis of the 'principal contradiction' in a specific conjuncture.[1] Likewise either class struggles or 'popular-democratic' struggles could predominate in political conflict. It is therefore essential to investigate specific state forms and particular political conjunctures in terms of their double determination through class and 'officialdom-people' relations. Indeed, although these twin determinations are analytically distinct, empirically they are bound to be closely intertwined and to condition each other in complex ways.

We can now consider the concepts of 'people' and 'class'. Whilst class relations are grounded in the relations of production, relations of political domination provide the basis for 'officialdom-people' relations. In this context the 'people' comprise those who are subject to state intervention and 'officialdom' comprises the agents of intervention. This implies a potential contradiction between them grounded in their differential political role and the nature of the ideologies that constitute them as subjects. The extent and form of class struggles in turn derive from the character of production relations and the interpellations that constitute economic agents into classes with different interests.[2] These processes of 'people' and 'class' formation are obviously closely related. Indeed, it is only with the full separation of 'state' and 'society' on the basis of capitalist relations of production, that the 'people' can be fully constituted in non-class terms and formally popular-democratic institutions be introduced (even if 'officialdom-people' relations and bourgeois democracy are both inevitably overdetermined by class relations).[3] In pre-capitalist class societies, on the other hand, the 'people' as such and political participation are alike formally structured in class terms. The significance of ideologies in determining the activities of classes as well as the 'people' as political forces should become apparent as we proceed.

The nature of 'democracy' and 'dictatorship' must now be defined. In its strong sense we can say that 'democracy' exists insofar as the 'people' and 'officialdom' are identical – because the separation between 'state' and 'society' has been transcended through the institution of self-government by the people. Moreover, since this separation is an essential precondition for the reproduction of class exploitation, 'democracy' in its strong sense also presupposes the abolition of the exploitation of one class by another. This is the classic position of Marx on true democracy and Communism.[4] But we can also define a weak sense of 'democracy'. This exists insofar as the 'people' are the 'principal aspect' (or dominant force) of the 'officialdom-people' contradiction. That is, although the institutional separation of the social formation into 'state' and 'society' persists, the 'people' are none the less able effectively to control the operation of 'officialdom' through specific mechanisms of representation and accountability. The most clear cut case would occur when the 'officialdom-people' opposition is dominant and/or the 'people' are constituted as an autonomous, unified political force. Conversely, to the extent that class relations constitute the principal contradiction and/or the 'people' form a heteronomous and/or disunified force, then democracy even in this weak sense would be correspondingly attenuated. But, as long as public officials were effectively subordinated to the 'people', it would be apt to describe state power in one of its determinations as 'democratic'.

In this context it should be emphasized that the absence of substantive democratic control need not entail the existence instead of a bureaucratic despotism or 'rule of officialdom'. For, although there is no real popular control of public officials, they may still be subordinated to other social forces and/or form a unified bloc with some such forces and/or themselves constitute the dominant class. Indeed, since effective control by an autonomous, unified 'people' in the context of a primacy of the 'officialdom-people' contradiction is exceptional, it is important to consider alternative forms of articulation between officials and other political forces. Of particular interest here are those forms of articulation that entail 'class dictatorship'. This would exist to the extent that 'officialdom' is directly subordinated to and/or unified with distinct class forces. The latter could comprise economically intermediate and/or subordinate class forces as well as forces representing economically dominant fractions and classes. Whether or not these different forms of dictatorship are consistent with the reproduction of the dominant relations of production cannot be determined from their class base but depends instead on the effects of the specific policies with which they are associated in a determinate conjuncture.[5] Finally, in addition to cases of direct subordination to and/or unification with distinct class forces, officials can also be indirectly dominated by such forces through the medium of control by the 'people' organized under the hegemony of a class force. In such cases we would have a weak democracy (characterized by heteronomy of the 'people' and the primacy of class relations) which acts as an effective, if indirect, form of class dictatorship (since the state is subordinate to class forces). It is with such cases of 'democracy' that we shall be most concerned in the following pages.

We have now presented a formal account of the principal terms for our analysis of the political contradictions of democracy. Two senses of democracy were distinguished: self-government by the people and the control of officialdom by the people. It has also been suggested that 'officialdom-people' relations are inevitably overdetermined by the relations among classes. This enabled us to distinguish varying degrees of democratic control ranging from the domination of an autonomous and unified people in combination with the primacy of 'officialdom-people' relations to domination by a heteronomous, massified people in combination with the primacy of class relations. In addition to these democratic cases we must also consider those cases where 'officialdom' itself is dominant or, alternatively, is subject to control by political forces other than the 'people'. Particularly important here are class forces but, once we shift from a class reductionist account and recognize the immense variety of political forces, other forms of political domination can also be discerned. In turn this implies that we cannot legitimately treat the state in a capitalist society as *ipso facto* essentially capitalist nor conclude that state power will inevitably assume the form of class dictatorship. This is especially clear when we examine the nature of democratic institutions in capitalist societies.

THE POLITICAL INDETERMINACY OF FORMAL DEMOCRACY

Lenin claimed that the bourgeois democratic republic was the best possible political shell for capital and thus that it was essential to replace it with proletarian democracy in the transition to socialism.[6] But it is far from certain that formal democratic institutions as such form the best shell for capital. Even a cursory glance at the various arguments advanced in support of this claim will reveal equally plausible counter-arguments. This suggests that there must be considerable indeterminacy in the democratic republic and that other forces must be present to ensure that it functions on behalf of capital. But, before the nature and operation of these other forces are examined, we should first present a brief account of this republic and its contradictions.

The bourgeois democratic republic is usually identified as a form of state in which parliamentarism is dominant and is then counterposed to the soviet system of conciliar democracy. It entails political representation mediated through the participation of 'citizens' in the policy-making of an elected government through their exercise of voting and related political rights and state intervention in the form of legislation or general policies enforced by a permanent rational-legal administration in accordance with the rule of law. This state form is then endowed with various functions in securing bourgeois domination.

As a system of representation it encourages the development of a unified 'power bloc' among dominant fractions and classes and it also facilitates the maintenance of hegemony over subordinate classes. Its function in the first respect is especially clear in the early stages of parliamentary evolution when the franchise was restricted and parliament was an important forum for representatives of various propertied interests to establish common needs, reach compromises, and formulate shared strategies. Moreover, as the franchise was progressively extended, the imperatives of electoral competition stimulated the main bourgeois parties to consider the interests of the dominated classes as well as those of the propertied. This provides one basis for the reformist politics necessary to maintain that 'unstable equilibrium of compromise' essential to bourgeois hegemony. Similar constraints discourage proletarian parties from promoting policies that are electorally unpopular and thus reinforce political moderation. In this context the emphasis on individual citizenship and the public or national interest also inhibits or undermines the development of strong class consciousness. To the extent that these electoral and ideological restraints are ineffective, the parliamentary-bureaucratic system still inhibits effective radical policies because of the separation of powers and/or similar institutional devices. Indeed the very separation of political representation and state intervention characteristic of a parliamentary republic performs significant functions in this respect. For it permits the smooth operation of the permanent administration while changes occur in the balance of forces in the representational field.

At the same time the system of rational-legal administration separates the masses from control over the means of administration and transforms them into its individuated subjects. For these subjects it none the less provides stable, calculable administration according to the rule of law in a *Rechtsstaat*; and, through its subordination to parliament, provides the means to change the law. This is especially appropriate during the phase of liberal competitive capitalism, when the principal role of the state is to secure the general external conditions of production and to restrict its more harmful effects through general legal or administrative interventions. It is also compatible with general macro-economic intervention through fiscal and monetary policies working indirectly through market forces (e.g. international tariffs, investment allowances, or contra-cyclical budgetary policies). Lastly, as such forms of intervention maintain the separation between the economic and political domains of capitalist society, they reproduce the dependence of the state on capital accumulation and so render it vulnerable to market forces and economic crises when its interventions prove inimical to the expanded reproduction of capital.[7]

Against such arguments that the parliamentary republic provides the best shell for capital, however, it is possible to offer counter-arguments that highlight its limitations and contradictions. For the bourgeois democratic republic is also liable to various political crises which restrict its abilities to function on behalf of capital and, even in normal circumstances, a number of dysfunctional consequences can occur. Thus its role in representation can be disrupted or paralysed through representational crisis marked by a split between the parties in parliament and their supporters in the country, a parliamentary crisis which makes cooperation among parties difficult or impossible, or a substantial penetration of parliament by forces committed to radical transformation of the relations of production and/or of political and ideological domination. Such crises may reflect and/or intensify difficulties in the electoral mediation of hegemony, the unification of the power bloc, and the bourgeois domination of parliament. These problems will be aggravated to the extent that parliament has effective control over significant means of economic intervention and/or is also confronting an economic crisis.

Dysfunctions may also be introduced through the normal operation of political competition. For adversary politics may encourage the abuse of executive power to secure electoral advantage at the expense of accumulation and/or lead to conditions in which long-term corporate planning becomes difficult owing to unpredictable changes in government policies. Again this involves most problems where the amount and scope of state intervention within parliamentary control is significant. For, as the state gains increased autonomy as a precondition of effective intervention to create, maintain, or restore conditions necessary to accumulation, it also gains the means to disrupt and undermine these conditions. This contradiction is aggravated by the fact that the requirements of capital in general cannot be fully determined *a priori* but often emerge only *post hoc*, if at all, as successive crises suggest that certain conditions of existence have not been realized. Thus an expansion in the scope and means of intervention need not be matched by an increase in knowledge about the methods and limits of their effective utilization. Indeed the technical nature, enormous scope, and discretionary character of new forms of state intervention can themselves result in the decline of parliamentary control over the administration branch at the same time as its activities lose their rational-legal, calculable character and escape from the rule of law. In return this could lead to a crisis of democratic legitimacy and/or to a bureaucratic despotism inimical to capital accumulation.[8]

Even this brief account of the effects of bourgeois parliamentarism should have established the political indeterminacy of democratic institutions. This is reflected in the historic struggles surrounding the introduction and extension of democracy and in the equally important struggles to eliminate or restrict democratic institutions in favour of political forms less hostile to bourgeois domination and accumulation. In part this indeterminacy is due to the hybrid institutional character of the state so that, even if a given state is organized under the dominance of parliamentary-bureaucratic institutions, other modes of representation and intervention remain possible.[9] In part it stems from the interaction between the parliamentary republic and constraints and forces located outside the political sphere, particularly those grounded in the process of accumulation. But in other respects it is due to the structured indeterminacy of formal democratic institutions themselves in relation to the constitution of political forces, their mutual relations, and the ends that they pursue in this context. This becomes clear when we re-examine the character of parliamentarism.

Parliamentary politics are mediated through the participation of 'citizens' in the policy-making of an elected government. Citizenship involves the institution of an individual juridical subject endowed with specific political rights and obligations and the extension of this status to all members of society without regard to their class or other attributes. Definite legal freedoms (such as freedom of association, freedom of speech, and free elections) are also required to enable the formal exercise of the citizen's rights of participation. It does not follow from the institution of citizenship, however, that the only legitimate political actors are individual citizens. Indeed the very freedoms entailed in citizenship provide the formal basis for the organization of many different political forces. In this sense pluralism is a typical feature of parliamentarism and it is this plurality of forces that constitutes the field of political struggle. This suggests the need for socialists not only to struggle for more democracy but also to base that struggle (and the struggle for socialism) on the existing system of forces. For, whilst freedom to organize and to exploit the indeterminacy of bourgeois democracy is essential to socialist advance, such advance is impossible without an adequate appreciation of the contending forces.

The struggle for democracy in this context involves struggle to extend the scope of citizens' rights of participation, to include more of the 'people' within the category of citizens, and to institute the legal conditions appropriate to democracy. Moreover, because formal democratic institutions do not in themselves guarantee substantive freedom and real popular control, popular-democratic struggle also encompasses struggles to establish and maintain the social conditions in which such freedom and control can be realized. The struggle for real democracy thus extends far beyond the narrow sphere of legal rights or the confines of parliamentary cretinism and involves the radical reorganization of all manner of social relations. In particular the realization of democracy requires the reorganization of the relations of production to eliminate class-based inequalities in political freedom; and the reorganization of relations in civil society to eliminate such inequalities rooted in relations among social categories.[10] This also implies the organization of the 'people' as a political force and its coordination with the class struggle. For, once the struggle for true democracy goes beyond juridical formalities to affect fundamental social relations, it can only be effectively pursued with the support of a broad-based mass movement. Conversely, for those forces wishing to confine the operation of formal democratic institutions in a bourgeois straitjacket, it is equally important at least to disorganize popular forces into a mass of mutually opposed groups and at best to organize the 'people' under their own hegemony. This suggests the provisional conclusion that the democratic republic is the best possible political shell for capital only when the bourgeoisie enjoys political hegemony.

CLASS FORMATION AND PEOPLE FORMATION

Our analysis has emphasized the importance of struggles to organize the 'people' in determining the effects of democratic institutions on bourgeois domination and capital accumulation. But the process of 'people formation' is far from adequately understood and needs further specification. Fortunately we are able to draw on recent theoretical advances in the analysis of class formation in order to illuminate the complexities of 'people formation'. Moreover, since the mutual relations among 'class' and 'popular' forces and struggles are also deeply problematic in Marxist political theory, it should be useful to examine class formation and people formation in the same political context.

It is a commonplace nowadays in Marxist theory that class determination (i.e. location in the relations of production) entails little about class position (i.e. stance adopted in class struggle).[11] This non-correspondence between class determination and class position suggests that *class struggle is first of all a struggle about the formation of class forces before it is a struggle between class forces*.[12] It suggests relations of production are not the objective basis for class formation in the sense of constituting singular and mutually exclusive 'classes-in-themselves' which necessarily develop sooner or later into 'classes-for-themselves'. Instead we must recognize that class schemata and class ideologies are themselves integral elements of the class formation process. Relations of production set definite limits to the success of particular class projects but they are typically compatible with various configurations of class forces. Within these limits the formation of distinct class forces is determined by specific struggles which have the organization and reorganization of such forces as their effect.[13]

The differential interpellation of economic agents as members of classes with common interests distinct from and/or opposed to the interests of other classes is therefore an integral element in the struggle over class formation and is overdetermined by the struggle to organize and give material expression to these classes. This is particularly clear in the case of intermediate classes such as peasants or the urban petty bourgeoisie and the positions that they adopt in class struggles. Indeed the political vacillations and instability of these classes is legendary in Marxist analysis. Moreover, although one cannot consider the bourgeoisie without reference to its inherent antagonism to the proletariat within the capital relation (whilst the class location of the traditional petty bourgeoisie has no necessary implications for its relations with other classes), it is none the less apparent that the struggle between bourgeoisie and proletariat also depends on the manner in which they are constituted as class forces.[14] For it is no more legitimate to reduce the class position of the main classes to their class location than it is for the other classes in capitalist society. For a certain indeterminacy of class position is universal.

It is this relative indeterminacy of class formation from class location that provides the essential space for struggles to establish class hegemony. The latter involves the interpellation and organization of different classes under the leadership of a given class (fraction) and depends on the specification and articulation of class interests in a manner that relates their satisfaction to the realization of the long-term interests of the hegemonic class (fraction).[15] Normally it involves a flow of material concessions to other classes and fractions and the sacrifice of certain short-term interests of the hegemonic class (fraction) and is thus conditioned and limited by the capital accumulation process. This hegemonization of class formation extends beyond the economic domain but its characteristic feature is the pluralization of class forces and their limitation to 'economic-corporate' demands. Indeed, since hegemony involves the realization of political and ideological interests as well as those linked to economic production, it is necessarily closely related to the articulation of popular-democratic demands and the formation of the 'people'.

The process of 'people' formation is analogous to that of 'class' formation. Thus, just as there is a non-correspondence between class location and class position, discrepancies also occur between location in the 'officialdom-people' relation and positions adopted in popular-democratic struggles. This indeterminacy likewise means that *popular-democratic struggle is first of all a struggle to form the 'people' before it is a struggle between the 'people' and 'officialdom'*. In turn this implies that, although those relations of political domination expressed in 'officialdom-people' relations set specific limits to the process of 'people' formation, the latter is finally determined by the differential interpellation and organization of political subjects as members of political categories with common interests distinct from or opposed to the interests of other categories. The state itself often plays an important role in the constitution of these categories. For its interventions interpellate and organize the 'people' into separate and mutually opposed categories according to the nature and purpose of these interventions. Indeed bourgeois law and rational-legal domination involve the constitution of subjects by their very nature.[16] This results in a myriad political categories – such as citizens, electors, taxpayers, welfare claimants, conscripts, convicts, aliens, and so on. The state itself is constituted as a sovereign legal subject and state officials are endowed with specific powers. Both state and officials may also be interpellated as servants of the people and/or responsible for the national interest.

At the same time political forces situated outside the state attempt to interpellate and organize these and other categories into popular forces in contradistinction and/or fundamental opposition to yet other civilian and/or official categories. Here one should remember that the articulation between 'officialdom-people' relations and class relations will influence the struggle to define popular forces and their antitheses. For, since it is extremely rare for 'officialdom' to constitute the dominant political force in autonomous fashion, its subordination to and/or unification with other forces can affect both 'people' and 'class' formation. Moreover, given the scope of state intervention and the necessity for state intervention against all civilian categories (and, indeed, its own officials) at some time, there is ample room for the most varied interpellations of popular and anti-popular forces. In this context the struggle to mobilize different categories and form them into a unified 'people' capable of dominating the state apparatuses constitutes the supreme focus of 'popular-democratic' struggles. But this process is also rather indeterminate.

This relative indeterminacy provides the space for struggles over hegemony in the field of popular-democratic politics. In this context hegemony involves the interpellation and organization of divers popular-democratic forces under the leadership of one such force (a party, mass movement, the military, etc.); and it depends on the specification and articulation of popular-democratic demands in a way that ties their satisfaction to the realization of the interests of the leading force. It should be emphasized here that the overdetermination of 'officialdom-people' relations through class relations influences the organization and maintenance of popular-democratic hegemony. Indeed, insofar as satisfaction of popular-democratic and economic-corporate demands depends on direct and/or indirect economic concessions, hegemony presupposes continued capital accumulation or continued movement to socialism. In this sense long-term hegemony must be based on, and articulated with, the exercise of a decisive function in the dominant or 'dominescent' mode of production.[17] In turn this implies that the struggle for hegemony revolves around interpellation and organization of class and popular forces in a manner that associates their alleged interests with those of the would-be hegemonic force and, at the same time, disinterpellation and disorganization of forces whose interests prove incompatible with such leadership.

The analysis so far might seem to involve a major contradiction. For it raises the question as to who struggles about the formation of classes and/or of popular-democratic forces if these struggles are prior to classes-in-struggle and people-in-struggle.[18] To the extent that this question does not simply rest on the genetic fallacy (i.e. class formation presupposes a 'class-in-itself' as a subject capable of self-formation and people formation presupposes as its originating subject a 'people-in-itself'), it can be answered in terms of possibilities inherent in the ever-pregiven nature of ideologies and relations of force. For, even if economic agents and political categories have to be formed into classes and popular forces rather than acting as such automatically on account of their class or popular location, they are not passive recipients of ideologies nor equally available for mobilization. Once we recognize that ideologies and ideological practices are ever-pregiven modes of signification of the real world that are liable to transformation and can transform that world, then we must also recognize that various developmental possibilities are present in any given ideology and/or its articulation with alternative ideologies and that such developments could transform or realign the prevailing relations of force. This is particularly likely during transitional periods and crisis situations.[19] Thus, whereas the class struggles during the transition to capitalism were influenced to a large extent by pre-capitalist ideologies, the latter were modified and transformed during the course of the struggles themselves. Likewise early popular-democratic struggles during the consolidation of the modern state or subsequent struggles during the transition to state monopoly capitalism are heavily influenced by the pre-existing communal or liberal ideologies. Both series of struggles were later transformed under the impact of new appraisals of the state, institutionalization of the changes in its apparatus and operation, alterations in the balance of forces, etc.

It should also be noted that class struggle does not presuppose the interpellation and organization of the forces in struggle immediately and explicitly as class forces. It is sufficient to merit the designation 'class struggle' that the struggles have determinate effects on the reproduction of the mode of production in question and then the class content of the forces in struggle will depend on the effects of their actions in a given conjuncture. This will often involve ambivalent and/or contradictory designations owing to the multiplicity of possible reference points for assessing the effects of such forces on reproduction.[20] This is apparent from a moment's reflection on anarcho-syndicalism, the Comintern, social democracy, Peronism, and left fascism as movements involved in class struggle. Nor, once it is conceded that class schemata and ideologies are themselves fundamental elements in the process of class formation rather than its superficial or epiphenomenal manifestations (and especially if we refuse to privilege the word 'class' and examine instead working concepts of class relations), can we adequately discriminate among class forces in terms of criteria like 'false consciousness' and 'fetishized consciousness'. An overall assessment must be related to the effects of various forces in struggle in a determinate conjuncture rather than to their supposed goals or professed self-image. It is for this reason that we stressed above that class struggle is first of all a struggle about the formation of class *forces* before it is a struggle between such *forces*. Even if the lonely hour of the last instance of 'pure class struggle' never comes, therefore, class struggle is omnipresent and one's strategy and tactics must be oriented to the existing balance of forces. This does not exclude attempts to realign and reconstitute these forces in order the better to conduct the struggle but it does mean that such attempts must themselves be related to the current situation.

It should also be clear that popular-democratic struggle no more presupposes the interpellation and organization of relevant forces immediately and explicitly as popular and anti-popular forces than class struggle requires that only 'classes-for-themselves' be in contention. However, rather than simply repeat the arguments of the last paragraph in a changed context, it will be more fruitful to draw out another implication. This implication is that all social forces are both class and popular-democratic forces. For, once we concede that class forces must be assessed in terms of their effects on the reproduction of social relations of production and that popular forces must be evaluated in terms of their effects on the reproduction of 'officialdom-people' relations, it follows that each and every social force must be located on both terrains of struggle. This has often been noted in connection with the reproduction of racial and/or sexual oppression in supposedly progressive class movements and the reproduction of class inequalities in popular-democratic movements. It provides a spurious justification for class reductionist analyses of all manner of forces and/or for the 'jacobin' analyses which exclusively emphasize popular-democratic perspectives.[21] And it constitutes a permanent rebuke for communists ignorant or oblivious of the non-democratic character of the Soviet bloc and other state socialist societies. It is to the analytical and political significance of this necessary duality of social forces that we turn in the following section.

THE DUALITY OF CLASS AND POPULAR FORCES

Various Marxist theorists have argued that the process of 'people formation' entails a process of 'class disorganization'. But is there really such a fundamental opposition between 'people' and 'class' that they cannot occupy the same political space or do these arguments involve the same class reductionist fallacy that we identified beneath the claim that the bourgeois democratic republic is the best possible political shell for capital? The answer to this question depends less on the different terrains relevant to 'class' and 'people' than on the compatibility or contrariness of the particular interpellations and/or organizational forms through which class and popular-democratic forces are constituted. In short, just as there is a certain degree of indeterminacy in the operation of democratic institutions, so too is there a certain indeterminacy in the relations of class and popular forces.

In liberal democracies the 'people' is legally constituted as the aggregate of individual 'citizens' entitled to participate in the processes of government decision-making and the state is presented as its point of public unity rather than as the focus of a determinate class unity.[22] However, even if this system of juridical interpellations has the effect of disorganizing and individuating the subordinate classes, it also has the effect of disunifying and massifying the people. This means that we are confronted with a *double process of disorganization*, that is, the disorganization of the people as well as of the subordinate classes. In this sense the process of 'people formation' confirms rather than contradicts that of 'class formation' and their common effect is the isolation or privatization of both popular and subordinate class forces. But the fact that the institution of universal suffrage and the circulation of commodities presuppose the formal constitution of 'free' individual subjects does not imply that other forces will be unable to develop and operate in this context. Indeed the exercise of hegemony typically depends on the existence of a plurality of popular-democratic and class forces whose interests and demands can be articulated with the realization of the preconditions of capital accumulation and bourgeois domination and, to the extent that this is not possible, on the reorganization, exclusion, or repression of the remaining antagonistic forces. Thus the process of *hegemonization also constitutes broad popular-democratic and class forces* through its orchestration of different interests and demands in response to changing circumstances so that an 'unstable equilibrium of compromise' is maintained.

In such cases the 'people' is formed as a broad, pluralistic, and heteronomous force, and subordinate class forces, even if they retain a certain autonomy, are confined within the limits of economic-corporate demands.[23] In this sense the effective reproduction of bourgeois hegemony presupposes at least a minimum degree of 'weak' democracy and it reinforces this through the successful designation of anti-capitalist and/or anti-state forces as sectional, undemocratic, disruptive, anti-social, and so on. This characterization is reinforced to the extent that these forces fail to develop a counter-hegemonic strategy linking popular-democratic and economic-corporate demands to a transition to a new social order. For, since it is capital that directly 'socializes' individual economic activities owing to its monopoly of coordination[24] and since it is the state that assumes ultimate responsibility for the public interest (even if both functions are overdetermined in performance through class and 'officialdom-people' relations), it is essential for an anti-capitalist and/or anti-state movement to articulate an effective alternative economic and/or political programme rather than simply adopting an oppositional strategy. Otherwise bourgeois forces could well monopolize hegemony or at least prevent its transfer to antagonistic forces during a crisis of bourgeois hegemony.

Thus it is through hegemony that the 'people' is formed as a unified force. This is not to suggest that the people must be completely unified and that no dissent or disagreement among them is permissible. Indeed it is an essential precondition for the maintenance of hegemony (as opposed to domination through a resort to force) that individuals and social forces are at least formally free to develop ideas and demands opposed to the prevailing consensus or 'equilibrium of compromise'. It is in this sense that formal democratic institutions facilitate the creation of hegemony. But such institutions must be complemented with the constitution of 'democratic subjects', that is, political subjects able to operate these institutions and engage in genuine democratic politics. In part this involves the realization of conditions in which formal freedoms can be exercised effectively but it also requires that the forces in question are willing to form alliances, to negotiate and compromise, and to subordinate private interests and demands to the public interest.

Although Marxists have recently recognized the important conflicts between 'capital in general' and 'particular capitals', there has been less recognition of those among 'labour in general' and 'particular labours' and among 'people in general' and 'particular peoples'. In this context the formation of a broad-based, inclusive movement of the people and subordinate classes does not rest on the satisfaction of each and every particular demand (especially as these are frequently inconsistent or incompatible); but depends on the ability to transcend certain of these demands through mutual sacrifice and/or their articulation with general interests. The exact incidence of economic-corporate or corporative popular-democratic sacrifices and concessions and the precise specification of the general interests are both important areas in the struggle for hegemony. For, while failure to reach compromises in the general interest could produce a crisis of hegemony, these compromises and dominant interests will determine what class and popular forces, if any, prove hegemonic and whether a transition to socialism or the reproduction of bourgeois order will result.

It is in this context that the articulation of popular-democratic and class forces becomes critical. For, since the social relations of production have definite political and ideological conditions of existence, transformation of the economy requires a corresponding reorganization of the state and ideological relations. But, since the state is the site of 'officialdom-people' as well as class relations, political reorganization involves the mobilization and/or neutralization of popular-democratic as well as class forces. Conversely, since the extension of democratic control requires the creation of specific material and social conditions favourable to the exercise of various formal freedoms, popular-democratic forces must also mobilize and/or neutralize class forces in the struggle to create these conditions. Thus, if freedom of communication or association is to be secured, changes will be required in the economic structure of the mass media or in the social distribution of free time. Likewise, if the economy is to be subject to democratic rather than bureaucratic planning, political representation must be restructured to permit the introduction of functional representation and its coordination with the parliamentary system.[25] The predominantly consensual reorganization of the systems of economic and political domination thus requires the close articulation of class and popular-democratic forces to form a broad-based, mass movement and to isolate the opposing forces and denude them of any popular support.

This conclusion is reinforced by consideration of the above-noted duality of class and popular-democratic forces. For, although certain social forces will be interpellated and organized principally as class forces, others as (anti)popular forces, and yet others as essentially non-partisan in either field of struggle, all social forces will inevitably have repercussions on class and 'officialdom-people' relations. It follows that socialist advance depends on involvement in both class and popular-democratic struggles and on their coordination and articulation so that the broadest possible mass base exists for the conjoint movement towards communism and democracy as well as for defence of existing achievements in these respects. Moreover, since all forces are involved in both class and popular-democratic struggles, it is essential that they are organized as far as possible to prevent internal perpetuation of class inequalities and relations of political and ideological domination. In all cases these struggles must be oriented to the current balance of forces (if only to reorganize it more effectively) and must assess the net effects of (non-)intervention in relation to long-term strategy and tactical considerations. Indeed, since conjunctures are inherently unstable and social forces develop in an uneven manner, constant reappraisal of institutions, interpellations, organizational forms, social forces, and conjunctures is required to enable appropriate changes in strategy and tactics. This applies just as much to the formal institutions of democracy as it does to other elements comprising the conjuncture. For the adequacy of the institutional mediations of democratic control is far from constant and reorganization of forms of political representation and state intervention may well be needed.

THE POLITICAL MEDIATION OF DEMOCRACY

So far we have treated class and people formation and the realization of democratic control of officialdom without regard to their organizational and/or institutional mediation. But the forms of organization are just as crucial to class and people formation as the nature of the interpellations involved; and substantive democracy depends not only on the presence of a 'people' but also on the mechanisms that ensure its effective representation and the accountability of public officials. Indeed, once the state is seen as a complex, hybrid institutional ensemble which has unequal and asymmetrical effects on the constitution of political forces and the scope and impact of intervention, then its reorganization is an essential element in popular-democratic struggles. At the same time, although the internal operations of the state make a major contribution to the overall coordination of official policies (especially in relation to the various conflicting and/or contradictory demands made upon it), it is also crucial to restructure the system of interest articulation and aggregation outside the state apparatus to encourage the formation of a more or less unified people. In both areas the range of appropriate and desirable reforms is large and we intend to provide only a few illustrations in these paragraphs.

Marxists have generally assigned the role of interest aggregation in the political sphere to the revolutionary party, which is in turn generally seen as organized according to the principle of democratic centralism. But, unless one is prepared to indulge in the class reductionist claim that the proletariat alone is revolutionary and that political parties are *the* political expression of class interests (which would still not solve the problem of the non-identity of proletariat and people), this is hardly a satisfactory account or prescription of the revolutionary political process. Indeed the need for the formation of blocs, alliances, and supporting tendencies was also recognized as an equally important aspect of revolutionary struggle; and the need for forging organic links with a wide range of mass movements was particularly emphasized by Gramsci.

In association with the functioning of the 'public sphere' in early liberal bourgeois democracies and of the institutional mediation of bourgeois power blocs in the more democratic state monopoly capitalist societies,[26] this suggests the need to develop a whole series of forums for public discussion and inquiry in which programmes and policies that transcend particular economic-corporate and/or corporative popular-democratic interests can be elaborated and confirmed. This applies not only to economic demands (where trades councils, soviets, internal commissions, etc., have played an important role in the coordination of demands in the interests of 'labour in general'); but also to popular-democratic demands (where the failure of the revolutionary 'public sphere' is more marked). In short the development of substantive democracy required the introduction of new forms of open, public discussion and inquiry in which individuals and organizations are free to participate and whose intended result is the formulation, coordination, and legitimation of economic and political programmes.

This must be accompanied by the reorganization of the state apparatus itself. Among the most important changes necessary here are the articulation of functional representation with the parliamentary system of representation, the democratization of functional and parliamentary representation, the maximum possible decentralization compatible with a coherent, coordinated political strategy, the transfer of administrative tasks to representative bodies, and the restructuring of the repressive state apparatus. First, since parliamentary representation formally based on the territorial aggregation of votes is increasingly dissociated from the nature and targets of intervention as the state acquires a wider range of economic functions, a system of functional representation must be developed so that those subject to intervention are directly and permanently represented. This requirement has often been expressed in terms of the need to replace bourgeois parliamentarism with proletarian conciliar representation. But this proposal ignores the need to articulate economic programmes and planning with the field of popular-democratic interests which are far less appropriately ordered through a system of workers' councils. Second, it is for this reason that determinate mechanisms of coordination or articulation between these two systems of representation are imperative.

Moreover, since neither the present parliamentary system nor the emergent functionalist system of corporatism are exactly democratic in function (even where they are democratic in form), the mere coordination of parliamentary and functional representation will not be sufficient to render the new system democratic. Both must be reorganized so that parties and 'corporations' are more democratic in their internal organization and in their orientation to general interests. Thirdly, while democratization demands a reversal in the tendencies to economic and political centralization, this must not prevent or inhibit effective coordination of programmes and policies to match the socialization of production and social life in general. It is here that the formation of a broad-based, unified 'people' is an essential precondition of substantive democracy since it permits decentralization to be combined with a coherent political and economic strategy. One aspect of decentralization would be the partial dissolution of the separation between officialdom and people through the extension of 'self-administration'. This would take the form of state intervention mediated through and/or delegated to 'private' organizations and associations; and/or the form of 'deprofessionalization' of official functions and their performance by individual citizens. Finally it would be necessary to democratize the repressive state apparatus in a number of ways.[27]

It should be emphasized here that institutional changes alone are insufficient to ensure the transition to socialism and democracy. For it would be just as erroneous to suggest that a reorganized democratic republic could guarantee this result as it is to suggest that the present democratic republic is essentially bourgeois in its effects. The early history of the Soviet Union contains enough lessons to make this caution unnecessary but it is unfortunately still essential to emphasize the structuralist or institutionalist fallacy that underlies such suggestions. In contrast we have argued that, just as the prevailing democratic republic is the best possible political shell for capitalism only on the condition that subordinate classes and popular forces are organized under the hegemony of the bourgeoisie, so does the socialist democratic republic require that class and popular forces will be unified into an autonomous people (or, during the transition, organized under the hegemony of the working class) capable of dominating the activities of 'officialdom'.

Lastly, lest it be forgotten and we be accused of overpoliticization of the transition or of voluntarism, it should also be repeated that the successful consolidation of hegemony depends on the articulation of economic-corporate and popular-democratic demands with the realization of the preconditions of capital accumulation (bourgeois hegemony) or with the successful transition to socialism and socialist democracy (socialist hegemony) and thus on the exercise of a decisive function in the dominant and/or 'dominescent' mode of production. But, as the Marxian alternative of 'the mutual ruin of the contending classes' or Luxemburg's stark choice of 'socialism or barbarism' suggest, the exercise of a decisive economic function is not in itself sufficient guarantee either of reproduction or of transition. Politics has its specific effects in both domains.

CONCLUSION

This paper has been principally concerned to develop an analysis of democracy that takes seriously the concept of a 'government by the people'. This requires a firm rejection of class reductionism but it does not warrant the rejection of all class-theoretical perspectives. Accordingly, although we established a firm analytical distinction between 'officialdom-people' and class relations, we also insisted on their close interconnection and overdetermination. Moreover, although we referred to a strong sense of democracy (characterized by the self-government of the people), we focused on the weaker sense of democracy (characterized by the control of officialdom by the people). This enabled us to distinguish varying degrees of democratic control ranging from the domination of an autonomous and unified people in combination with the primacy of 'officialdom-people' relations to domination by a heteronomous, massified people in combination with the primacy of class relations. The development of democracy in these cases depends on the formation of a broad-based 'people' and on specific organizational and institutional means of representation and accountability. The absence of these conditions is associated with more open forms of class dictatorship and/or with bureaucratic despotism. This makes it imperative to examine the process of class and people formation and the organizational and institutional mechanisms of formal democracy. These were the issues whose examination comprised the greater part of the paper.

We therefore considered the alleged effects of bourgeois parliamentarism and attempted to demonstrate the political indeterminacy of democratic institutions. In themselves they cannot guarantee capital accumulation or bourgeois domination and, indeed, in certain conjunctures they can create and/or reinforce crises of accumulation or domination. It is this indeterminacy which accounts for the critical role of class and people formation in determining the effects of democratic institutions. Our analysis of these processes began with the artificial separation of class formation from people formation but then moved on to stress that, since it is class *forces* and popular *forces* rather than classes or the 'people' as such that are formed through such processes, there is a close connection between them and a necessary duality of social forces. This became most evident when we considered the creation and consolidation of hegemony as the mobilization of popular-democratic and economic-corporate forces through linking their various demands and interests to the continued accumulation of capital and the maintenance of the bourgeois state or, alternatively, to a successful transition to socialism and socialist democracy. This invites the inference that *hegemonization constitutes the 'people' as a social force through the organization of both class and popular forces* and that the 'people' is a central concept for the analysis of social formations in the same way as 'class' is for the study of modes of production. And, since it is at the level of social formations that the state and politics (and, indeed, class formation) are situated, their analysis must be centrally concerned with the 'people' as well as with class forces.

Finally we presented a brief and truncated discussion of the political mediation of democracy. This emphasized the need to reorganize the existing institutions of parliamentary democracy and to develop an array of public forums to facilitate the formation of a unified, autonomous people.

One of the major problems confronting the struggle for socialism today is that socialist forces are not organized to exploit the opportunities offered by the political indeterminacy of bourgeois democracy and are tempted to attribute its strengths to its institutional forms alone rather than to reconsider their own political strategies and tactics. But this does not justify the alternative conclusion that a change in strategy and tactics will be sufficient to secure the socialist millennium within the framework of existing institutions. For, in addition to the limits imposed by the failure to engage in the struggle for popular hegemony (and, indeed, the apparently systematic abandonment of the field of popular-democratic struggle to the right), there are also limits imposed by the separation of political representation from state intervention and the institutional separation of the political domain as a whole from that of economics.

Thus, just as it is essential to transcend the confines of parliamentary cretinism and narrow economism in order to form a 'people' unified through a shared commitment to socialist democracy, it is also imperative to transcend the separation of representation and intervention and the overarching separation of politics and economics. Only in this way will it prove possible to secure the institutional conditions most favourable to the transition to socialism and the creation of a socialist democracy.

To conclude, it is worth considering the extent to which economic and political conditions in state monopoly capitalism are being transformed through the dynamic of capital accumulation itself in ways that favour as well as inhibit the struggle for socialism. In particular, although state monopoly capitalism is associated with a tendential decline in parliamentarism, this creates the conditions for hegemonizing the struggle for democracy and linking its realization to a transition to socialism. Moreover, whilst parliamentary democracy may well be in decline, functional representation is in the ascendant. This form of representation is significant because it has initiated the movement to transcend the separation between representation and intervention along with that between politics and economics. Admittedly, corporatism effects this within the limits of the capital relation (just as Marx indicated that the joint-stock company represented the abolition of private property within the framework of the capital relation); but corporatism also provides an important new arena of struggle for socialism on a terrain that is more favourable in certain respects than the liberal parliamentary-bureaucratic state. In this sense corporatism also embodies the contradictions of bourgeois democracy but it incorporates them in a more acute fashion. This is not to suggest that state monopoly capitalism is the 'threshold of socialism' and will automatically evolve into socialism. It is to emphasize that the process of capital accumulation continually changes the conditions of struggle, and recent developments have reinforced the indeterminacy of bourgeois democracy. Indeed the combination of international economic crisis and the emergent crisis of democratic institutions has stimulated a veritable flood of anti-democratic bourgeois propaganda and programmes. This presents socialist forces with opportunities to reassert the popular-democratic heritage of socialism and to isolate bourgeois forces in this field as well as in that of economics. These opportunities should be welcomed.

NOTES

1. Mao Tse-tung introduced two important distinctions into dialectical materialism in order to help specify the particularity of complex phenomena and their contradictions: (a) the 'principal contradiction' is that which determines or influences the nature and development of other contradictions and (b) the 'principal aspect' of a contradiction is that pole which plays the principal and decisive role in its development. Neither the principal contradiction nor the principal aspect are pregiven and permanent but they can change with the conjuncture. Clearly these are essentially heuristic concepts which can sensitize us to a range of phenomena that might otherwise be neglected but they cannot substitute for concrete historical investigations. On these concepts, see Mao Tse-tung, 'On Contradiction', *Selected Works*, vol. I, Foreign Languages Press, Peking, 1967, pp. 311–47.

2. The importance of ideological interpellations in determining the nature of popular and class forces has been emphasized respectively by Ernesto Laclau and Adam Przeworski. See E. Laclau, 'La Teoria Marxista del Estado y el Pensamiento Latinoamericano', unpublished paper, 1978; and A. Przeworski, 'Proletariat into a Class: the Process of Class Formation from Karl Kautsky's *The Class Struggle* to Recent Controversies', *Politics and Society*, 7 (4), 1977, pp. 343–401.

3. Cf. E. B. Pashukanis, *Law and Marxism*, Ink Links, London, 1978, pp. 139–40 and *passim*.

4. Cf. K. Marx, 'Contribution to the Critique of Hegel's Philosophy of Law', in K. Marx and F. Engels, *Collected Works*, vol. 3, Lawrence and Wishart, London, 1975, pp. 3–130.

5. This implies a radical displacement of theoretical focus in studies of state power, from the search for guarantees that the state apparatus and its functions are necessarily capitalist in all aspects, to a concern with the many and varied contingent effects of state power on accumulation and political domination in determinate conjunctures.

6. Lenin, 'State and Revolution', in Lenin, *Selected Works*, vol. I, Progress Publishers, Moscow, 1963, p. 296.

7. The ideas in this paragraph are developed at greater length in B. Jessop, 'Capitalism and Democracy: the Best Possible Political Shell?', in *Power and the State*, ed. G. Littlejohn *et al.*, Croom Helm, London, 1978, pp. 10–51; further references will be found there.

8. ibid.; see also B. Jessop, 'Corporatism, Parliamentarism, and Social Democracy', in *Corporatism in Liberal Democracies*, ed. P. Schmitter and G. Lehmbruch, Sage, London, 1979.

9. Although it is commonplace nowadays to emphasize the hybrid character of economies as a complex articulation of mode(s) of production and forms of social and private labour, there is less recognition to the hybrid character of the state: it

involves a complex articulation of forms of representation and intervention and this results in a complex space of political manoeuvre in all forms of state.

10. See B. Jessop, in *Power and the State*, op. cit., p. 14; and Laclau, 'La Teoria Marxista del Estado y el Pensamiento Latinoamericano', op. cit.

11. In addition to the paper by Przeworski, see N. Poulantzas, *Classes in Contemporary Capitalism*, New Left Books, London, 1975, pp. 13–35; E. O. Wright, *Class, Crisis, and the State*, New Left Books, London, 1978, pp. 36–110; and A. Cutler *et al.*, *Marx's* Capital *and Capitalism Today*, vol. I, Routledge and Kegan Paul, London, 1977, pp. 167–312.

12. Przeworski, op. cit., pp. 371–3.

13. ibid., pp. 367 et seq.

14. Laclau has drawn a sharp distinction between 'class struggle' and 'classes-in-struggle': the former is immanent in the concept of a mode of production based on class exploitation, the latter is contingent on the articulation of modes of production. But, to the extent that this implies that the class position of classes involved in 'class struggles' is also given (whereas that of classes involved in 'classes-in-struggle' is contingent), this argument and distinction is just as fallacious as other attempts to deduce class position from class determination (see E. Laclau, *Politics and Ideology in Marxist Theory*, New Left Books, London, 1977, pp. 104–7).

15. A. Gramsci, *Selections from the Prison Notebooks*, Lawrence and Wishart, London, 1971, pp. 55–90, 158–75, 206–70, and *passim*.

16. Pashukanis, *Marxism and Law*, op. cit., *passim*; and Edinburgh CSE Group, 'The Crisis of the State and the Struggle Against Bourgeois Forms', mimeo, 1978.

17. Gramsci, *Selections from the Prison Notebooks*, op. cit., p. 161.

18. Przeworski, op. cit., pp. 386–7.

19. Laclau, *Politics and Ideology in Marxist Theory*, op. cit., pp. 102–4; Gramsci, *Selections from the Prison Notebooks*, op. cit., pp. 210–23.

20. There are various conditions of existence of accumulation at the economic, political, and ideological levels; there are problems in assessing short-, medium- and long-run effects; there are various alternative courses of development of accumulation; and so on.

21. Laclau distinguishes 'jacobinism' from other moments in the popular-democratic struggle in terms of the acquisition of popular-democratic elements of the maximum possible autonomy from class overdetermination and its presentation of the 'people' as a political alternative to the existing system of domination (*Politics and Ideology in Marxist Theory*, op. cit., p. 116).

22. Cf. N. Poulantzas, *Political Power and Social Classes*, New Left Books, London, 1973, pp. 276 et seq.

23. Gramsci emphasized that hegemony presupposes the autonomy of subordinate classes and groups as a condition of organizing the 'unstable equilibrium of compromise' in relation to changing conditions: see C. Buci-Glucksmann, *Gramsci et L'Etat*, Fayard, Paris, 1975 (English translation, Lawrence and Wishart, 1980), pp. 73–5; and A. Sassoon, 'Hegemony and Political Intervention', in *Politics, Ideology, and the State*, ed. S. Hibbin, Lawrence and Wishart, London, 1978, pp. 9–39, especially 14–15 and 30–1.

24. Cf. D. Wells, 'The State as Fetish: a Marxist Analysis', unpublished paper, 1978.

25. Jessop, 'Corporatism, Parliamentarism, and Social Democracy', op. cit.

26. On the 'public sphere' in early liberal democracies, see J. Habermas, *Strukturwandel der Öffentlichkeit*, Luchterhand Verlag, Berlin, 1962, *passim*. For a good review of the institutional mediation of power blocks in the USA, see A. Szysmanski, *The*

Capitalist State and the Politics of Power, Winthrop, Cambridge, Mass., 1978, pp. 228–35.

27. I freely admit to the weakness of this statement on the RSAs and hope to return to this question in subsequent work; for a view that would be critical of that contained above, see P. Anderson, 'The Antinomies of Gramsci', *New Left Review*, 100, 1977, pp. 5–80.

GRAMSCI: A NEW CONCEPT OF POLITICS AND THE EXPANSION OF DEMOCRACY

Anne Showstack Sassoon

From the time Marx criticized Hegel's view of the state for its inability to provide a theoretical basis for unity between society and politics, a central theme in Marxism has been the expansion of democracy as part of the transformation of the relations of production. The concrete difficulties of building socialism in the Soviet Union and other countries and the inability of these countries to develop democratic control by the masses has been an important element in the debate over whether it is, in fact, possible to develop a third alternative which goes beyond both the limitations of social democracy (as a version of liberal democracy) and those of so-called 'real' socialism, or 'socialism as it actually exists'.[1]

A variety of political forces in Western Europe and elsewhere maintain that such an alternative is possible, and we are witnessing the expansion of a discussion about the relationship between democracy and socialism. Central themes in this discussion are the protection and expansion of individual liberties and the coexistence of different political parties in a socialist transformation of society. Yet if this discussion is not to remain at the level of an assertion of ideals, if the link between socialism and democracy is not to be defined merely in terms of a tactical necessity, any notion of the expansion of democracy as an integral aspect of the transition to socialism must derive from an analysis of the contradictory reality of the development of capitalism itself.

In order to approach this immensely difficult task, we must be clear about the necessary point of departure. Any analysis of the *forms* of state and the concrete development of the forces of production must begin with an analysis of the social formation. This approach will allow us to consider the forms of the relationship between economics and politics, and between the mass of the population and the political and economic spheres. Indeed the development of the forces of production is inscribed within a struggle for hegemony in which in the modern epoch of the organization of the masses and the dominance of monopoly capital there is an historically *novel* relationship between the state and society, between the public and the private.[2] As the state intervenes in all aspects of peoples' lives, old notions of the division between economics and politics, between the public and the private are open to discussion.

It is only by examining these changes that we can begin to analyse the possibilities of new kinds of political and social movements, such as the women's movement, and their relationship to an expansion of democracy and a transition to socialism. The yardstick by which to determine whether these new forms of political intervention will constitute an aspect of the *transformation* of a traditional relationship between rulers and ruled is not their mere existence in an organized form. The hallmark of *any* kind of modern state is the organization of the masses, be it liberal democratic, fascist, or socialist.[3] The measure which can indicate whether organizational forms and specific demands contribute to a new concept of politics, rather than simply representing an element of passive revolution in which capitalism is reorganized,[4] derives from the historical project which is on the agenda for the first time, the establishment of a new type of state through the political protagonism of the masses, expressing an intellectual and moral reform rooted in a transformation of the economy.

The crucial theoretical contribution for investigating this subject is that of Antonio Gramsci. Running through his work is a discussion of the new relationship between masses and politics, between changes in the economic sphere and the possibility of a social control over the economy. According to Gramsci, it is because of changes in the period of organized capitalism[5] that possibilities are presented for the institution of popular democratic control over the sphere of politics. This is a *real* rather than a utopian project because changes in the organization of production provide the basis for a new relationship between the masses and knowledge with immense consequences for science and philosophy.

Gramsci's notes on philosophy must be read in the context of posing the problem of the transformation of forms of knowledge and the acquisition of intellectual skills by *masses* of people rather than by the small elite who have up to now had a monopoly of knowledge. These changes in social knowledge or forms of rationality are an integral aspect of changes in the forms of political *power*.[6] The massification of the intellectuals and the new relationship between intellectual skills and the productive process which are the results of changes in the economy are one aspect of the way in which the very reorganization of capitalism produces elements for the transition to socialism, a transition itself conceivable only as a process.

The organizing thread in the whole of Gramsci's writings is a new concept of politics, adhering to the possibilities of the new age, a concept which is able to conceptualize an expanded democracy, the socialization of politics based on social control over the economy. Starting with Marx's discussion of the abolition of traditional politics based on class differences and reflected in the specialization of political activity,[7] Gramsci provides elements with which to answer those critics who claim that the project of abolishing politics is utopian. He goes beyond Marx in his development of tools with which to think the transformation of politics and its complement – a new concept of philosophy – rooted in the reality of the development of the present social formation.

Because the theme of a new concept of politics does indeed inform the whole of Gramsci's work, I would like to consider here just a few aspects: first, his criticism of liberal democracy and his discussion of the crisis of liberal democratic institutions; second, his argument about the possibility of a new social control over the economy, rooted in the development of the forces of production; and third, his writings on the political party.

Gramsci's criticism of liberal democracy is not a criticism of representative institutions *per se*. The question, according to Gramsci, was rather whether new forms of representative democracy could be created[8] which provided for a real unity between the masses and the political sphere. For it was the inability of liberal democracy to provide for this kind of control, because politics was separated from the socio-economic reality of the mass of the population, which was the basis of Gramsci's criticism.[9] The crisis of the liberal state was, Gramsci said, a crisis of hegemony and had two interrelated aspects.

In the period of the organization of the masses and increased state intervention in the economy, control over politics was being subtracted from traditional institutions.[10] Parliamentarism, parliament as a talking-shop, denounced by a wide range of commentators, was a manifestation of the inadequacies of the traditional liberal democratic institutions, rooted in a concept of the state as separated from economics, in a period in which the state began to intervene increasingly in all areas of society and had to bargain with organized groups. A variety of solutions to the crisis of liberal democratic institutions were being offered in the 1920s and 1930s. Corporatism in various forms was promoted as reflecting the reality of the power of organized groups and of providing a more adequate system of representation.[11] Continuing to the present, many writers have claimed that classical liberal notions – such as that of J. S. Mill of individual political participation as a civic virtue and an asset to society – are dead, and that the necessary and sufficient condition of a democratic society is competition between elites or between pressure groups.[12]

Gramsci's response was to go beyond the traditional terms of the question of democracy by analysing the contradictory effects of the crisis of liberal democracy. An aspect of this crisis was the possibility of the development by the working class of a new type of social-political control, rooted in production. In the period 1919–20, Gramsci saw the beginnings of a new concept of politics in the development of the factory councils. According to Gramsci, the factory councils were the organizational forms which enabled workers to go beyond the definition given to them by capitalism, as wage labourers, divided according to skills from each other and subject to the anarchy of market relations. In his articles in the *Ordine Nuovo* Gramsci wrote that through their participation in the factory councils, which unified the whole of the work force in a factory, workers could realize themselves as *producers*, part of a whole productive process, united as a class and uniting various sectors of society through a new relationship between political, economic, and social roles.

The worker as producer was a political actor not simply because of a formal-legal definition of him as a citizen but because as part of a collectivity he was able to intervene to control the economy and control the state.[13] The preconditions of this kind of transformation, one of epoch-making proportions, were being provided by capitalist development itself, by the organization and concentration of workers in the factory, by the changed relation of capital to the productive process in which the figure of the individual entrepreneur was declining and the role of finance capital and the state was increasing, and by the long-term inability of the capitalist social formation to guarantee an expansion of the productive forces in general.

Gramsci does not have a crisis theory of the *collapse* of capitalism, but rather, a theory of the survival and reorganization of capitalism *through* crises. The long-term crisis of capitalism continually challenges all old relationships; it constantly reshuffles the cards. The precise forms of the transformation of social relations, the way in which the pack of cards was redealt, depend on the nature of the political intervention of the various forces in the field.

It was in this field of crisis that Gramsci defined the proletarian revolution as a revolution made by the masses which develops the forces of production and founds a new type of state reflecting an intellectual, moral, and economic reform. It may seem surprising given the wide variety of superstructural interpretations of Gramsci, which argue that the essence of Gramsci's writings lies in his consideration of culture and ideology but that he has little to say about the economy, but a close reading of his work both before and after he was imprisoned shows that he emphasized constantly the *unity* between transformations in the economy and the rest of society. This unity was conceived in terms not of a *reduction* of different levels to changes in the economy, but rather in terms of the need to pose the possibility of a transformation of society within the context of the potential given by changes in the organization of production.

Indeed it is Gramsci's view that the precise delineation of the connections between changes in production and the organization of society was determined through a struggle between rival hegemonies rather than *predetermined* by any simple causal relationship that leads him to substitute the notion of 'historical bloc' for the metaphor 'base and superstructure'. Changes in the organization of production and in the relationship between the state and the economy provided the possibility for overcoming the division between manual and intellectual labour, for making real a *social* control over the economy. This implies that it is now conceivable to assert the primacy of politics over economics. Based on an expansion of democracy, a social political control over the economy can be substituted for the anarchy of the market forces which has hitherto prevented a rational social control over politics and the whole of society. The qualitatively different nature of the hegemony of the working class and of the historical bloc it struggles to realize is to be found in the expansion of democracy in which the mass of the population can for the first time in history increasingly establish control over social development – the masses can act as historical protagonists.[14]

From this brief presentation of some general indications of the way Gramsci linked changes in the social formation with the creation of an expanded democracy, I would now like to focus on a rather specific aspect of his work – his discussion of the revolutionary party. In doing this I am not attempting a general analysis of Gramsci's work on the party[15] but I want to consider his work on the party as one of the areas which reflect his concept of politics and his investigation of the dimensions of an intellectual and moral reform and the problems which must be considered in any discussion of the expansion of democracy.

For Gramsci the party is a collective organism born in this social formation but whose object is to break through it, paralleling the function of the working class itself. In this sense it has to provide organizational forms, but, more centrally, it has to create a process of politics which reflects the qualitatively new task of the working-class movement – it must be a 'school of State life'.[16] The historical project of the working class, the founding of a new type of state, requires a new type of political party.[17]

In the debate about democracy and pluralism taking place throughout Europe, it has been argued that a party which is truly committed to democracy must reflect this democratic vocation in its internal organization. Specifically it is claimed that democratic centralism contradicts a commitment to democracy which can only be *insured* by the existence of factions. The question which must be posed is whether democracy is in fact maintained by a system of guarantees, of formal rules and formal structures. However important the rules are, and they are important, any *reduction* of the concept of democracy to a set of guarantees in fact prevents the posing of the very real problems involved in protecting those democratic institutions and practices which exist today against any threat of authoritarianism, and inhibits the conceptualization of the concrete problems presented by an expansion of democracy. This kind of reduction is rooted in a concept of politics which cannot conceptualize the protagonism of the masses, and it is only by political activity by the mass of the population that democracy can be protected and expanded. One of the richest sources of indications for studying the problems involved in the creation of a full democracy are Gramsci's writings on democratic centralism and party organization.

But first, a warning: from his earliest writings, in his argument against the limitations of the Italian Socialist Party (PSI), Gramsci is quite clear that the party does not provide the *form* of the new state, which can only develop from the experience of the mass movement and which has no previous model.[18] Moreover, for Gramsci organizations as such are related to their function and to the nature of society. Therefore, while we will find a discussion about the internal relations of the party which constitutes an important contribution to the debate on the development of democracy, there is no one-to-one relationship of precise forms of organization. The organization of the state is not reducible to the organization of the party. The two have similar but not identical tasks. The task of the party is to create a strategy, to act as a collective intellectual in forming new concepts which go beyond those provided under capitalism, for a social transformation made by the masses under the hegemony of the working class. The new type of state reflects an historical bloc made up of a variety of forces not all of whom are organized in a single party or parties. What *can* be found in Gramsci's writings on the party is a discussion of the process of politics which has parallels for the process of politics in the state.

Gramsci defines the Modern Prince, the revolutionary party, in terms of its task: to found an integral state based on a fully extended hegemony, deriving from a collective will and reflecting an intellectual and moral reform. Gramsci's silence on precise forms of organization is significant. The lack of specific indications about both party and state rules must be read in terms of a specific notion of politics, that notion which is adequate to the historical potential of the modern epoch, when the mass of the population becomes organized in a multitude of forms and thus acquires the potential to intervene in politics for the first time – to become protagonists in history. We find a constant insistence in Gramsci's writings, from the time of his debate with Bordiga, that organizational questions are *political* problems and cannot be treated as absolutes.

Gramsci writes that parties are 'schools of state life' whose internal mode of politics reveals their view of the state and of society.[19] From the time of the *Ordine Nuovo*, he argues that in the period of the transition to socialism, in which the problems of building a new state with a new project (the political realization of the protagonism of the masses) becomes real and concrete, that party whose aim is to create a new *type* of state must itself be a new *type* of party.[20] The internal organization of this party must be appropriate to the way in which what Gramsci calls the fundamental problem of political science is posed: that there is a division between leaders and led – a fact which cannot be ignored – and that the questions which are now historically real are the following:

How can this split be overcome?[21] How can there be a democratic, a hegemonic relationship between leaders and led?[22] How can a real, an organic unity, a collective will be forged in the period of the protagonism of the masses?

These are the questions which are reflected in the internal life of the party.

Now the problem of the division between rulers and ruled and the difficulty of creating cohesion in a society marked by competition and diversity are problems which are posed by bourgeois political thought from Hobbes to the present. Hobbes, who attempts to construct a theory adequate to the society developing out of the breakdown of feudal relations, portrays atomic, separated individuals who accept obligation to a sovereign in order to create a legal order to guarantee the conditions in which they may compete. The process of politics is defined by Hobbes as a *set of rules* or channels within which competition can take place. Within Hobbes's vision there is no intermediary between the individual and the state and no positive bond between individuals.

Locke's response to the possibility of a tyrannical state is to reserve the maximum of power in the hands of individuals and to limit the state in an argument expressly designed to take account of the needs of private property. Social cohesion, the needs of society as a whole, it is *assumed*, is an automatic byproduct of a social order based on individualism. This was expressed later by Adam Smith with the phrase, 'the hidden hand', which moved behind the multitude of individual decisions to produce the optimal result for society as a whole. The state is viewed as separated from the economy, and its sphere of activities is severely limited. Starting with Hobbes, but more precisely expressed by Locke and classical liberal political and economic thought, this separation of state from society and the economy provides the ideological underpinnings for the so-called 'nightwatchman state'.

Rousseau and Hegel are struck rather by the lack of cohesion in bourgeois society. In order to overcome strife while maintaining the essential features of that society, Rousseau's 'general will' is based on individualism and assumes the impossibility of the formation of groups. The relation between individual and state remains unmediated. The concept of private property is maintained, and the state is in varying ways 'mystical', that is, a preconstituted entity which is not the product of the intervention of human subjects but which, it is assumed, provides for all. Hegel's concept of the 'ethical state' which constitutes the highest achievement of rationality for society is based on a view of the bureaucracy as an élite removed from the conflict between groups.[23] It is not coincidental that we find in different forms implicit or explicit references to this notion of a state which intervenes to 'improve' society by groups of intellectuals who have a traditional élite relationship to the mass of the population: the Italian neo-Hegelians, like the Spaventas or Croce, and the Fabians are only a few examples. Even when the task of the state expands, if real control over politics and economics remains beyond the grasp of the mass of the population, the bourgeois notion of politics remains unchanged. Old forms of hegemony are put into crisis only to be substituted by new forms of organizing society which maintain a separation between the political sphere and democratic control by the masses.

What is a central question in liberal thought is what is termed the problem of political obligation. This is the ·vay the relationship between the individual and the state is conceptualized. To the extent that this relationship of separation between the mass of the population and control over economics and politics is maintained, whatever socio-political and economic changes take place, crucial aspects of the social relations of capitalist society are not overcome, but are simply reproduced in new forms. Gramsci describes this with the concept 'passive revolution'.[24]

Later in the last century and in the period in which Gramsci was writing, a number of thinkers reacted to what had become an increasingly obvious feature of society – the organization of the masses. Some, like John Stuart Mill, attempt to construct a system of constraints to prevent the civilized minority from being overwhelmed by the powerful but as yet uneducated majority. Others, considering the new forms of organization, such as Robert Michels, with his theory of the iron law of oligarchy,[25] assume as historically permanent the split between leaders and led and argue that bureaucratic and oligarchic forms of organization are proof that the extention of democracy is impossible. The political consequences of the organization of the masses and the expansion of the activities of the state were thus the object of investigations within bourgeois thought. Those Marxists who were interested in these developments, like Bukharin, tended to consider them in a unilateral way, posing the question of the *economic* effects of state intervention without seeing that the economic and the political were in a new relationship in which they each had to be conceptualized differently.

This is where Gramsci's thought represents a break not only with bourgeois political philosophy but with the thinking of both the Second and Third Internationals. Gramsci poses this question of leaders and led and of the unity and cohesion of society in a particular context in which the very question of leaders and led and of the unity and cohesion of society is transformed. If we read his notes on party organization, we find in fact a constant redefinition of words which are themselves related in a new way. This is an aspect of Gramsci's *rethinking* of certain organizational terms which is symptomatic of his attempt to rethink politics in general.

First of all, democratic centralism is defined in terms of the creation of a true democracy as the only way to relate to a constantly contradictory and changing reality.[26] Secondly, centralism or the creation of unity is only real and effective to the extent that the organization is democratic;[27] and democracy is possible in so far as there is a process of discussion and debate which ensures a constant raising of the intellectual and political level of the mass of members.[28]

It is this preparation, this moral and intellectual reform, which enables the individual to appropriate reality, to act as an autonomous subject as part of a collectivity. The necessary organizational condition for this to be accomplished, according to Gramsci, is the establishment of an intermediate stratum between the rank and file and the leadership, which thus are linked through a *mediated* rather than a direct relationship, by a chain which is based on a division of labour, on what Gramsci calls *technical differences*, rather than 'class divisions', implying that there is no innate difference between the different levels which cannot be overcome through a process of acquiring intellectual skills.[29] Thus, all members of the party must be considered intellectuals.

This in turn is related to Gramsci's redefinition of the nature of the skills of the intellectual. The term intellectual is redefined and broadened to enable it to comprehend the unity of theory and practice, of mental and physical labour, so that the intellectual and moral reform of the masses can be conceptualized.[30] Gramsci says that all men always use intellectual skills, but only some perform the function of intellectuals in society, a function which Gramsci described in terms of organization as well as intellect, broadening the category to include all those who organize hegemony in political and civil society, from civil servants to factory technicians, from school teachers to social workers, etc. The way in which intellectuals relate to the mass of the society, in so far as they provide the hegemonic 'cement' for that society, signals the type of relationship which exists between leaders and led, between state and society. What Gramsci calls the organic intellectuals of the working class must express a new 'mode of existence', a new democratic relationship with the masses in which the division between mental and physical labour begins to be transformed.[31] Citing his experience with the *Ordine Nuovo*, Gramsci argues that the basis for this transformation already exists in the most recent developments of capitalist society.[32]

Gramsci defines the very meaning of unity in a particular way. If it is not the result of positive consent and active participation, it is like 'a stagnant swamp', a situation in which, to change to a metaphor used by Marx, the individuals relate to each other as in a sack of potatoes.[33] It is this lack of positive cohesion, this separation between individuals and between groups which is a hallmark of bourgeois society. For Gramsci, a true collective will in the party and in society as a whole, united around a qualitatively new project for society, cannot be established through the imposition of a unity based on a passive relationship between leaders and led, as conceptualized in bourgeois political thought.

Yet this unity is not uniformity according to Gramsci. His concept of hegemony, for example, implies the creation of unity based on compromises between different social forces organized in a variety of ways. In terms of the party, unity takes account of the different opinions of the members of the party which relate to different interpretations of reality. Gramsci argues that discipline whose origin is not the result of a democratic exchange and debate in fact reproduces the political divisions in bourgeois society, because the attitude to the leaders becomes one of faith in which the individual feels extraneous to the outcome of any situation, or separated from reality. That is, what a group of leaders does, or the results of a party's policies are not understood as the product of the active intervention of *each* party member, but appear independent of rank and file activities.[34] A relationship of faith between rulers and ruled represents a delegation of power from the ruled to the rulers, thus reproducing the liberal schema of,

(1) the rulers as protectors of a pre-established order, and,
(2) the ruled as separated from politics, enclosed within a private world.

Gramsci's redefinition of terms is made necessary by the very task of the party: to ensure an organic relationship between leaders and led, to realize the political protagonism of the masses. Without this democratic relationship inside the party and between the party and the mass movement, the party is ineffective because its politics inevitably fail to relate effectively to a constantly changing and complex reality. Nor does its internal life reflect a new concept of politics.

There are various implications in this approach. First of all, a fully democratic relationship cannot be defined by a set of rules but only by a mode of conducting politics based on realizing the protagonism of the masses and aimed at the abolition of the division between leaders and led. If this is to be accomplished then *links* between individuals and the state, or between leaders and led are necessary if the divisions which exist are in fact to be overcome.[35] If the real organizational, political and cultural problems enabling the masses to appropriate reality and to participate in politics are not confronted, then the appeal to the masses, according to Gramsci, is in fact pure demagogy, whether this appeal is by Mussolini or any other political leader. New problems of organization are constantly posed related to the changing situation, both for the party and for society at large. This is the logic of Gramsci's argument that there can be no abstract rules of organization since organizational forms are always related to a concrete situation, to political questions and crucially to a concept of politics.[36]

Various objections to this comparison of Gramsci's discussion of the party and the creation of a fuller democracy in society at large may arise. It has been noted that Gramsci assigns enormous tasks to the party.[37] In fact, he claims that the attempt to have a set of ideas gain acceptance over the mass of society is a feature of *any* party. In competition with other ideas any political force seeks the greatest support it can muster. While it may seem that Gramsci leaves little space for the autonomous activities of other parties and non-party organizations, and while it is true that he does not explicitly discuss pluralism, the coherence of the whole of his thought provides a theoretical basis for thinking the problems of political representation and political forms, and consequently pluralism.[38] This concept of hegemony implies the need for the working class to relate to different social and political forces, that is, to take account of differences and to seek to overcome the divisions of society which are reinforced by bourgeois social relations through unification around a new project. But to refer to our discussion above, this unity must be on a democratic basis. And we must be clear that Gramsci's concept of hegemony refers to the hegemony of a class and not to the hegemony of a party. At the same time there is nothing which guarantees the longevity or success of a political force which is not able to represent the needs of an epoch.

Gramsci's criticisms of the PSI and of Bordiga's view of the party are relevant here. The PSI, he argued, was an ineffective instrument for a fundamental change in society because it reproduced the bourgeois mode of politics, in particular the split between economics and politics – for example, in the division of labour it established with the trade union movement. Its internal organization provided for debate but not a true democracy or unity of action. The lack of *theoretical* discussion prevented it from understanding concrete reality. The split between leaders and led remained within the party and no effort was made to go beyond a formal definition of citizens unrelated to their socio-economic position.

Attempting to overcome these features, Bordiga's solution as the first leader of the Italian Communist Party (PCI) merely reproduced them.[39] His concept of rigid centralization in fact resulted in a lack of effective cohesion, reproducing the split between leaders and led and between human subjects and reality. Without having an active relationship to the creation of the strategy of the party and thus a creative relationship to reality in day-to-day activities in a flexible development of tactics, the rank-and-file, Gramsci says, will not understand that analysis of the current situation which is the basis of a certain set of policies, and while they might pay lip-service to the party line, this line will not in fact be effectively translated in their daily political intervention.[40] In turn, the rank-and-file through their day-to-day activities provide the actual links to reality and to the experiences of the mass movement to which the party's programme must constantly relate and against which it must be tested.[41]

Gramsci argued that Bordiga's schematic view of organization in which a certain pattern of organization is assumed as universally valid, is related to a mechanical view of history in which the organization itself is abstracted from the historical process, a philosophy of history which in fact cannot conceptualize the protagonism of the masses. Indeed this mechanical view of history was the common theoretical foundation underlying the organization of the two parties, the PSI and the early PCI, a view which was shared with bourgeois thought.[42] Organizations and events seemed to exist without the active intervention of human subjects, and the party, as the state, appeared as a mystical creation separated from the activity of the individual members. Economism in its various forms is unable to postulate a basis for effective political intervention by the masses. It thus reproduces the commonly-held notion that history is beyond the control of human subjects.

Parties where the leadership have an instrumental relationship with the mass of the members, that is, which do not reflect in their internal life the problem of the realization of the protagonism of the masses, reflect an aspect of the *passive revolution* in that the traditional relationship between leaders and led is reproduced while at the same time providing for the organization of the masses on a new basis.[43] In this context Gramsci was most directly concerned with analysing the fascist party. Yet, to the extent that the relationship between leaders and led remains that of bourgeois society, the party in question, with whatever ideology and in whichever social formation, cannot provide real democracy or the organic exchange between rulers and ruled, however democratic the rules themselves. Thus Gramsci provides us with indications for an analysis of the lack of an effective democracy in a variety of parties, in capitalist or socialist countries, and indeed in non-party organizations as well.

But what about Gramsci's criticism of factions? In terms of his direct discussion, a problem arises in that most of his writing on the topic is to be found in his articles and party documents produced in the debate against Bordiga and his factional activities in the period 1924–6 during the consolidation of the fascist regime. Yet, there is a general argument against factions which we can derive from Gramsci's various discussions. This argument is related to the fact that the revolutionary party must have an organizational form which enables the working-class to unify itself and to create a strategy which overcomes the splits in bourgeois society. It therefore needs unity of action in which there is a constant interchange of ideas, discussion, criticism and personnel between the various levels of party organization but in which divisions are not concretized in *formal organizational* terms. Indeed, Gramsci argues that the only assurance against factional activity lies in an effective internal democracy in which debates are undertaken in the spirit of arriving at an accurate understanding of reality and an effective strategy and tactics.[44] The existence of factions in fact hinders this object because the conflict tends to express itself in terms of organization versus organization or personality versus personality rather than around different sets of ideas.

In any case it is quite clear from Gramsci's work as we said earlier that the *form* of the state is not to be reduced to the *form* of the party even though the party's view of state and society is reflected in the party's internal life. Gramsci writes that in one-party states the party in fact loses its direct political function. 'The political function is indirect. For, even if no other legal parties exist, other parties in fact always do exist and other tendencies which cannot be legally coerced.'[45] This elimination of pluralism reproduces what Gramsci calls bureaucratic centralism, in which it is impossible to achieve a collective will, a positive unity, a true democracy because 'political questions are disguised as cultural ones, and as such become insoluble'.[46] This is a criticism of totalitarian states and totalitarian parties which applies not only to fascist Italy but also to Stalinist Russia.

At the same time the existence of several parties is not itself a guarantee of pluralism and the further development of democracy. Dramatic examples would be South Africa or indeed several of the socialist countries, but in addition a wide range of literature from a variety of theoretical positions has also criticized the quality of pluralism and the limits of democracy in countries like Britain or the United States where the 'rules' are undoubtedly democratic in a formal sense. The rules are a necessary premiss, the importance of which no one should underestimate, but formal democratic guarantees are incapable of in fact guaranteeing an interest let alone participation in politics.[47] While a generation of political scientists and sociologists have theorized a defence of apathy,[48] the nature of the proletarian revolution necessitates full, active, continuous participation by the mass of the population. In the transition to a new society as the masses organize themselves politically, the multitude of possible forms of pluralism manifest themselves as the problems and limits of liberal democracy are constantly being revealed. At the same time the vast problems to be encountered in making real an expanded democracy – problems having to do with the organization of people's lives, the divisions to be overcome, and the organization of knowledge – present an enormous challenge.

If the revolutionary party is to provide the concepts and the strategy for the working class to think through the problems of an expansion of democracy, the party itself, in its internal process of politics, must create the kind of interchange between leaders and led which is rooted in a new concept of each member of the party as an intellectual, reflecting the potential for an intellectual and moral reform presented by new developments in capitalist society. Gramsci's new concept of politics is related to his view of these developments as having contradictory effects, as challenging the old ideas and old institutions of liberal democracy while providing new opportunities for the working-class movement. But new opportunities, such as a dramatic decrease in the working week stemming from vast changes in productive methods – a necessary

premiss for a real and effective participation by the mass of the
population in politics – could simply constitute an aspect of the passive
revolution in which capitalism reorganizes itself on a new basis, in this
example, with an enormous increase in unemployment, if the working
class and its organizations do not analyse the changes in capitalism in
their contradictions. A political strategy which breaks through the logic
of capitalist relations of production must be rooted in these
contradictions, in the reality of the capitalist social formation, in order to
go beyond it to build socialism.

NOTES

1. In Italy this debate has mainly concerned Bettino Craxi, Secretary of the Italian
   Socialist Party (PSI) and other socialist and so-called 'lay' intellectuals who maintain
   that there is no alternative, and on the other hand the numerous statements and
   articles of Italian communists who maintain that a 'third way' is possible. But in fact
   the question is a central aspect of debates about and within Eurocommunism.
2. Here we would have to disagree with the argument that present-day state intervention
   is nothing more than what the state has always done, e.g. with the poor laws (see for
   example Mary McIntosh, 'The State and the Oppression of Women' in *Feminism
   and Materialism*, ed. by Annette Kuhn and Ann-Marie Wolpe, London, Routledge
   and Kegan Paul, 1978). The way in which the state now underwrites investment in all
   advanced capitalist countries represents a politicization of a crucial area of economic
   activity, once left in the hands of autonomous capitalists answerable to nothing but
   market forces. Moreover, massive state intervention in the private sphere, for
   example in education which until the end of the last century was not even
   conceptualized as a socio-political responsibility, means that relations between
   individuals and the state and between individuals in civil society are articulated
   differently. The mode of this articulation is increasingly political.
3. The right, for example, has usually been more aware than the left of the potential of
   women in politics. Often appealing to specifically female and at times feminist
   themes, women have been organized in an anti-progressive manner in a number of
   countries at crucial moments in their history. See Donatella Venturi, *I golpe delle
   donne. L'uso reazionario della questione femminile in American Latina*, Bari, 1978.
   In fact women are often more effectively organized by the right because traditional
   roles are less challenged. Examples would be the Conservative Party in Britain and
   the Christian Democrats in Italy (see Simona Maffei's perceptive essay, 'Le siciliane',
   in *Essere donna in Sicilia*, Rome, 1976).
4. Gramsci's concept of passive revolution is important in order to understand that the
   strategy which the working class movement undertakes in the war of position must
   be qualitatively different from that of the bourgeoisie. We return to it below.
5. Non-Marxists have been in no doubt that this period represents something
   historically new. There were wide-spread debates in the 1920s and the 1930s about
   the increasing need for the state in advanced capitalist countries to bargain with
   organized groups. In an unpublished paper Robert Skidelsky points out for example
   that the Treasury was well aware that this would be a consequence of a more
   interventionist policy in their debates with Keynes in the 1920s. Another aspect of

the developments in capitalist society which was widely discussed was the changed role of intellectuals. To consider just one more example, in his interesting if idiosyncratic book, *The Revolt of the Masses*, Ortega y Gasset takes up many of the themes of the challenge to traditional liberalism represented by the presence of masses who now consider that they have the right to intervene in history.

6. This is a theme developed by Giuseppe Vacca in an unpublished paper, 'La teoria del socialismo in Gramsci'.

7. Implicit or explicit in Weber's discussion of politics as a specialized activity related to the development of bureaucracy and more recent work on the relationship between knowledge and power, such as that of Foucault, is the notion that politics, and the organization of knowledge, is inevitably the activity of the few. Gramsci suggests that the very development of capitalism provides the basis for a new concept of politics related to a new organization of knowledge. He thus also goes beyond Sorel's criticism of the role of intellectuals, and he touches on several of the themes considered by the Frankfurt School although within a very different problematic.

8. See Antonio Gramsci, *Selections from the Prison Notebooks*, London, 1971, pp. 193–4, and pp. 255–7 (cited hereafter as *Selections*).

9. Antonio Gramsci, *Selections from Political Writings, 1910–1920* (hereafter cited as *Political Writings, 1910–1920*), London, 1977, pp. 73–4. In this article Gramsci differentiates his views from both the syndicalist position of complete rejection of the terrain of politics and the traditional Socialist Party acceptance of the terrain as given. The assumption of politics as an unchanging activity underlay both positions.

10. ibid., p. 76.

11. G. D. H. Cole's work on guild socialism is one example. See also Adrian Lyttelton's account of the debates which went on in Italy in the 1920s about the institution of a corporate system, *The Seizure of Power, Fascism in Italy, 1919–1929*, London, 1973. A traditional theme in Marxist views of the state has been the inadequacy of parliament to control the state.

12. Going back to Schumpeter's book, *Capitalism, Socialism and Democracy*, London, 1961, first published in the 1940s, and continuing with the work of such people as Robert Dahl, *A Preface to Democratic Theory*, Chicago, 1956, this has been a particularly strong tendency in American political science, and attacked in turn by Peter Bachrach, *The Theory of Democratic Elitism*, London, 1969, to mention only a few works in what has become a vast literature about the problems of liberal democracy.

13. This is a theme discussed by Nicola Badaloni in several different works, most notably *Il marxismo di Gramsci*, Turin, 1975. Gramsci's conception is different from Sorel's because rather than suggest a retreat into the economy abandoning the political sphere as innately the terrain of the bourgeoisie, Gramsci suggests an advance into politics based on a transformation of working class politics and politics in general. See *Political Writings, 1910–1920*, pp. 65ff, 73ff, 98ff, 103ff, 109ff.

14. Vacca, op. cit., discusses the effects of changes in production on changes in the relationship between manual and intellectual labour. Badaloni discusses the notion of the establishment of a social control over the economy and a new concept of individual freedom in 'Attualità di Gramsci', in *Attualità di Gramsci*, edited by Mario Spinella, Milan, 1977, and in 'Libertà individuale e uomo collectivo in Gramsci', in *Politica e storia in Gramsci*, vol. I, edited by Franco Ferri, Rome, 1977.

15. In the following section I am drawing on material developed in my book *Gramsci and Politics*, forthcoming, London, 1980. Many of the arguments which follow are more fully illustrated and analysed there.

16. See *Selections*, p. 269.
17. See *Political Writings, 1910–1920*, p. 76.
18. See *Political Writings, 1910–1920*, pp. 142–6, especially, p. 144.
19. See *Selections*, p. 26.
20. See *L'Ordine Nuovo, 1919–1920*, Turin, 1955, pp. 141–2, and *Political Writings, 1910–1920*, pp. 73ff.
21. See *Selections*, p. 144.
22. That the hegemony created by the working-class movement must be democratic is implicit in the whole of Gramsci's work, but several of the points I have been making are found in the following passage: '*Hegemony and Democracy*. Among the many meanings of democracy, it seems to me that the most concrete and realistic one must be connected with the concept of "hegemony". In a hegemonic system, democracy exists between the leading group and the groups which are led, to the extent that the development of the economy and therefore legislation, which expresses that development, favours the (molecular) passage from the groups which are ruled to the ruling group' (*Quaderni del Carcere, I–IV*, Turin, 1975, p. 1056).
23. For a discussion of the theme of bureaucracy in Gramsci's work and how it compares and contrasts with the writings of Hegel and Marx on the subject, see Luis Razeto Migliaro and Pasquale Misuraca, 'The Theory of Modern Bureaucracy', in *A Gramsci Reader* edited by Anne S. Sassoon (forthcoming, London, 1980).
24. I trace the development of the concept of the passive revolution in my book *Gramsci and Politics*, op. cit. See also Christine Buci-Glucksmann's article in *Gramsci and Marxist Theory*, edited by Chantal Mouffe, London, 1980, and the article on the passive revolution in *A Gramsci Reader*, op. cit.
25. Michels develops this theory in *Political Parties. A Sociological Study of the Oligarchical Tendencies of Modern Democracy*, London, 1962, first published in 1915, which was based in large part on an examination of the German Social Democratic Party. Gramsci's critique of Michels is to be found in *Quaderni del Carcere*, pp. 230–239.
26. See *Selections*, pp. 188–90.
27. See the note 'Passato e presente. Centralismo organico e centralismo democratico. Disciplina', *Quaderni del Carcere*, op. cit., pp. 1706–7.
28. See for example, Antonio Gramsci, *Selections from Political Writings, 1921–1926*, London, 1978 (cited hereafter as *Political Writings, 1921–1926*), pp. 197, 290, 364, 367, and footnote 22 above.
29. This argument is one aspect of Gramsci's criticism of Michels.
30. See *Selections*, pp. 8–10, 12–13.
31. This is the sense of the passage on p. 10, ibid. The new 'mode of existence' of intellectuals is a crucial aspect of an intellectual and moral reform.
32. See *Selections*, pp. 9–10, 12, 13.
33. See *Selections*, p. 190; the reference is to a quotation from Marx's *Eighteenth of Brumaire of Louis Bonaparte*.
34. See *Quaderni del Carcere*, op. cit., pp. 1769–71, and *Selections*, p. 187, footnote 83.
35. For Gramsci's discussion of the need for these links in the party see *Selections*, p. 153. Also relevant are his notes on 'The Theorem of Fixed Proportions', ibid., pp. 190–2.
36. One of the most important aspects of creating an expanded democracy is a change in the ways peoples' lives are organized, between work and leisure and in the division of labour now existing between the sexes. If we are to go beyond the Third International notion of the 'professional revolutionary' and the bourgeois concept of politics as

separated from the private, then on a very concrete level the mass of the population must have the time, energy and intellectual preparation to intervene in politics as a normal aspect of their everyday lives.

37. Massimo Salvadori, among others, has recently claimed that Gramsci has a 'totalitarian' notion of the task of the party. See 'Gramsci, and the PCI: Two Concepts of Hegemony', in Mouffe, op. cit.

38. My argument here is that Gramsci's discussion of politics as necessitating compromises with a variety of groups in which the hegemonic force goes beyond a corporatist view of its role, plus his general interest in the modes of organizing the masses in the modern period, provide the premises for focusing more specifically on questions of the forms of representation of political forces. The use by Gramsci of the term 'nomenclature of a class' to indicate the way in which parties represent classes is not particularly helpful, however. For a development of a discussion on these questions, see Palmiro Togliatti, 'La concezione del partito politico della classe operaia', *Togliatti, Opere scelte*, Rome, 1974, pp. 1147ff, especially p. 1149.

39. See *Political Writings, 1921–1926*, p. 290.

40. See for example, ibid., p. 197.

41. This is a theme which runs throughout his debate with Bordiga and is also central to his work in prison.

42. See *Quaderni del Carcere*, op. cit., pp. 749–51, pp. 1706–7, and *Selections*, op. cit., p. 187, footnote 83.

43. It is because of the qualitatively new task of the proletariat that it cannot simply use an existing élite of intellectuals for its own purposes but must change their relationship to the mass movement. These 'traditional' intellectuals can perform functions organic to the creation of a new social formation only if they, too, undertake an intellectual and moral reform. And the intellectuals formed through the revolutionary party are organic intellectuals of the working class only if they succeed in relating to the masses in a new way, which is not automatically the case simply by belonging to a party which considers itself revolutionary (see *Selections*, p. 187).

44. See Antonio Gramsci, *La costruzione del partito comunista, 1923–1926*, Turin, 1971, p. 161.

45. See *Selections*, p. 149.

46. ibid.

47. For example in the 1978 mid-term elections in the US approximately 34 per cent of those registered to vote did so – and far less than 100 per cent of those who are eligible to vote are even registered. Other examples are low participation in trade union elections, in local government elections, etc., in Britain.

48. This is what Seymour Martin Lipset does for example in *Political Man*, Glencoe, Ill., 1960.

REVOLUTIONS, REFORMS OR REFORMULATIONS? MARXIST DISCOURSE ON DEMOCRACY

Colin Mercer

I. THE POLITICAL CONTEXT

This contribution takes as its starting-point the notion of a 'Third Way' to socialism − between Stalinism and social democracy − which has emerged most markedly from a political and theoretical debate which has been going on in France, and more especially in Italy, for some time now.[1] First used in the present debate by the Italian communist Pietro Ingrao (generally acknowledged as the spokesperson for the left of the Italian Communist Party − PCI), it was taken up by others after him and has, to a certain extent, become a watchword for those on the European left who have been concerned to bring Marxist theory and practice out of a pervasive and disabling set of dichotomies.

There is a very obvious sense in which the notion of a 'Third Way' is itself inadequate since it can suggest that politics is simply a matter of a number of clearly available 'choices'. But however inadequate in the theoretical sense, the term none the less serves to designate an engagement with the nature of revolutionary strategy in the advanced bourgeois democracies and an attempt to avoid the associated dichotomies of either the traditional social-democratic forms of integralism and reformism, or the 'jacobinism' and authoritarianism implicit in 'models' based on the Soviet experience. In Italy the debate became more intense during the summer of 1978 when several leading politicians and theorists of the Italian Socialist Party (PSI) questioned the ability of the PCI to govern whilst it retained, among other things, its 'Leninist' heritage and democratic centralism as a principle of organization. These two central targets were related in turn to other equivalences and oppositions: Leninism *versus* pluralism, Leninism *equals* totalitarianism, and so on − a familiar discourse of political and theoretical options which it will be part of the project of this contribution to interrogate.

These simple equivalences and oppositions which, for very good reasons, are easily recognizable by all involved in debates and struggles over the nature of socialist strategy, were the main terms in the more opportunistic part of the debate which filled the Italian papers for some time. And in its own terms, the attack hit hard and had the desired effects. But this political moment has to be seen in the context of a longer-term debate within the Italian left where the questions have been posed in a more principled way, or rather, where certain 'obvious' questions about whether this or that is 'reformist' or 'revolutionary' were themselves being interrogated.

At issue in this have been three major areas; the nature of the state, the political forms of transition, and the necessity for an integration, far from automatic, of *democracy* within that process. In this contribution, I will attempt to interrogate the discourse of the political moment by drawing on some of the developments of the theoretical moment: an interrogation of the options offered by a Marxist discourse which has tended historically to be structured around the apparently immutable conceptions of 'reform' and 'revolution' which, I believe, have been radically disabling in their political *essentialism*.

In France the situation is somewhat different though the themes are similar. If, in Italy, the debates were taking place within the prospect of a future communist-socialist government, the terms of the debate in France are rather more tinged with bitterness and disappointment following from the failure of the Union of the Left to gain a majority in the governmental elections of March 1978. This failure sparked off a dispute not only between the communists and the socialists but also within the parties themselves, and most intensely within the French Communist Party (PCF). Louis Althusser's critique of the strategy, structure and ideology of the PCF[2] contains direct political allegations concerning the role of the party in the pre-election period but also, and more important for us, raises the theoretical failures which Althusser locates within Marxism as a whole. These failures, or, more correctly, 'absences'[3] within Marxist theory link up with the debate in Italy, and it is in the sense that these debates overflow with *implications* (not applications) that I want to examine some of the theoretical points of reference which go beyond purely national conjunctures. This is not an attempt to reject one set of 'models' and propose another, but it is an attempt to locate and displace certain dominant and sterile dichotomies structured around the pervasive 'alternatives' of revolution and reform and to suggest certain *reformulations* which now, more than ever, are crucial for the construction of new political and theoretical terrains for struggle.

II. THE THEORETICAL CONTEXT

The problem is not one of simply offering new political choices. There must also be an accompanying theoretical reconstruction to displace the constantly recurring dichotomy of 'reform or revolution'. This, I believe, is what Antonio Gramsci was acutely aware of both in his political practice and his theoretical work, and much of the argument of this contribution owes a great deal to some of Gramsci's formulations in his *Prison Notebooks*.

One of Gramsci's proposals in these writings which, I would argue, is extremely pertinent to the need for a theoretical reconstruction within Marxism, was an analysis of the linguistic and cultural metaphors used by Marx, including those of 'base' and 'superstructure'.[4] Unfortunately, this work was never carried out, but his proposal, and Gramsci's attention throughout his work to what he termed the 'immense philological labour' required in the reading of any body of theory, and his awareness of the political and material effects of language, can provide a suggestive starting-point for a necessary engagement with the current 'crisis of Marxism', involving both a political critique of existing practices and a critique of the epistemology which informs them. This does not involve a series of questions about 'what went wrong' or what other choices were or are available, but it does involve questioning the discourses which generate certain 'obvious' choices and deny others. This also involves the disarticulation of certain 'necessary' correspondences which exist within Marxist theory between certain concepts and propositions. It is in this sense that I want to examine the *discourse* of reform and revolution, of alternatives and oppositions affecting the idea of democracy within Marxism, and not the alternatives and oppositions themselves.

Any discourse, constituting a certain perspective on a certain field of objects, is structured around key metaphors and motifs which have the power to evoke and connote a certain set of meanings and possible actions, and to deny others. 'Revolution' and 'reform' have tended to function like this in the history of the communist and socialist movements

– as metaphors with certain sets of associations for many disputes on strategy and transition. And even when these terms do not come to the fore, their related effects are present. To a large extent we are still very much *within* this discourse though much has been done over the recent period to displace its central tenets. We are frequently faced with a situation of simple alternatives and oppositions – either this or that; if you do this then it will inevitably lead to that; this particular feature is a classic example of this or that model, and so on. And these 'alternatives' are not simply self-sustaining; they interact with other concepts and propositions in Marxist theory from many different directions: with certain conceptions of base and superstructure, of the relation between economics and politics, the nature of the state, etc. They form a pervasive substratum of connotations, a 'grammar' of the left which, in the absence of anything else, will constantly return us to old ground, preventing the realization and creation of new terrains on which to struggle. This particular 'grammar' defines what another Italian communist, Umberto Cerroni, has called the 'maximalism-reformism scissors' which, he argues, must be rejected if we are organically to recompose 'a unified horizon of theoretical definitions'.[5]

It is in this sense that the problem is both epistemological *and* political and demands not that we simply look back to past 'errors' which can be corrected but that we understand that these were also part of a pervasive discourse in which we are still, to varying degrees, situated. The problem at the theoretical level then becomes one not of adding something to a progressively evolving body of work called Marxism, but of closely examining the sets of connotations and correspondences and re-articulating them to compensate for the 'absences' engendered in the accepted paradigm.

This discourse of reform and revolution is usually accompanied by a certain conception of power where power relations are visible and obvious in their sites of concentration. Power is located there to be either 'seized' or 'managed'; by frontal attack or step by step occupation of the existing structure. Within this model there are two possible forms of democracy; formal (and therefore bourgeois) or direct (and proletarian). What this means in effect is that power relations and the subsequent forms of democracy are elaborated in terms of empirically-observable sites of dominance which are simply substituted in the new order. History becomes the history of simple domination structured around 'obvious' institutions of repression and subordination; democracy becomes the *inevitable* outcome of the removal of those institutions.

This, in varying degrees, has been the dominant interpretation within the Marxist tradition. But if it has been dominant, it has not been exclusive: the concept of *hegemony* both as a strategic and as a theoretical principle stands as a critique of this model of power relations, designating both the complex nature of existing relations of forces and the possibilities of their transformation. In this sense the concept of hegemony becomes an index of democratic transition.

Hegemony serves as this index in so far as it suggests that the history of bourgeois democracies is not understandable simply as a history of repression but also, as Gramsci indicates, a history of the complex generation of spontaneous and 'active consent'. A certain conception of democracy has been central to this process; generated at many levels – culturally, personally, juridically – and not just in the 'formal' terms of the purely political domain of the representative apparatus. It is in terms of this extended concept of power relations implicit in the concept of hegemony that I want to examine the meaning of democracy at a later stage; this will involve a brief consideration of some of the work of the French philosopher Michel Foucault from whom I have taken the concept of 'power relations'. Foucault is not a Marxist, but his work on the nature and mechanisms of power in Western bourgeois states, his refusal to theorize these simply in terms of what he calls 'the effect of obedience', or a 'juridico-discursive' conception, is close to the forms of analysis now being undertaken by Marxists under the rubric of 'how the ruling class rules' – the cultural, ideological, political, epistemological forms of existence of specific hegemonies in specific national conjunctures. For Foucault, the history of bourgeois states is not just one of repression, but of multiplication, dispersal and diffusion of power relations extending even to a certain codification and location of sexuality, to conceptions of the function of the mind and the place of the body, the location of the 'soul' and of 'consciousness' – in short, of the human ideological subject.[6] This is another area in which I will attempt to trace the meaning of democracy.

Connected to this integration of Foucault's power relations with the Gramscian concept of hegemony is a *relational* theory of state power proposed by Nicos Poulantzas in his most recent book, *State, Power, Socialism*.[7] Against any notion of the state as 'object' or 'instrument' to be either smashed or manipulated, Poulantzas argues that the state must be understood in relational terms in so far as, especially today, classes cannot be considered as somehow 'outside' the state in a relation of exteriority, but are within the state. But if the subordinate classes are within the state, they are not there on their own terms. The gaining of civil and democratic rights in popular struggles over a long period are not just concessions on the part of the ruling class, they are genuine, but not isolated gains which affect the *form* of the state; but none the less the subordinate class is retained in a position of exclusion because the apparatuses of power are not neutral and simply manipulable. In the processes of the historical formation of these hegemonic apparatuses, that is, in the history of the bourgeois states, specific forms of domination will have been materialized and inscribed in institutions and the ideological discourses which intersect them (school, family, asylum, cultural forms, etc). It is in the acknowledgement of this initial dissymmetry of the presence of the masses within the state and the complex forms of their presence there that any strategy for a democratic transition to socialism has to start. And this transition is to be located in that untheorized and 'open' space which we can attempt to approach through an examination of some definitions of democracy and their place in the Marxist tradition.

III. DEFINITIONS

The definition of democracy is a dificult task if we consider the diverse writings on the subject from Plato, through Hobbes and Locke, Kant and Rousseau to Marx and Lenin. In his book *Keywords*, Raymond Williams, with an eye to the importance of the generation of *meanings* for the existence of any ideology, takes about four and a half pages to attempt some sort of location. What emerges is a word with multiple meanings and an astonishing historical variability ranging from 'obeying no master but the law' to 'popular power'; from the various combinations of 'formal democracy' and 'representative democracy' to 'real', 'direct' or 'people's democracy'.[8] That there is no clear definition is not just a question of words or semantics but also one of history – a history also of the creation of meanings. And since we do not make up our own meanings, this history and its very real residues and traces will have specific effects and implications on our thought and actions.

In varying contexts the word democracy has had decisively different meanings and political implications. And what is more important is that since the emergence of the various bourgeois representative states, the word democracy has been articulated with a great number of other words and meanings; the juridical subject, the free, ethical individual, the 'neutral' sexual subject, the householder and so on. Intersecting with all of these and finding a connotative relationship with them, democracy must be considered more than a 'formal' device imposed from above by the dominant class; it is inscribed and materialized within the hegemonic apparatuses and in the ideological subjects produced in and through them. The formation of bourgeois hegemony requires this complex diffusion of meanings and practices; a process indicated by Gramsci in his formulations on the 'integral state' (coercion plus hegemony) which I will discuss below.

Before about 1850 in England, the word democracy was more or less synonymous with 'blood on the streets' or the 'rule of the mob', as the spokesman of the ruling class looked nervously back to the French Revolution. Within the remarkably short space of about ten years it had changed its meaning, being incorporated, with the spread of the democratic franchise, educational reforms, etc., within the discourse of the ascendant liberal state, which now saw the need to become a liberal *democratic* state. As a word and as a concept it of course predated the liberal state and will go beyond it, but it is important to register that precisely because meanings are neither free-floating, nor fixed, democracy takes its place in the hegemony of the British state through a process of negotiation and articulation. The new meaning of democracy in the nineteenth-century British state was not just an act of will on the part of the bourgeoisie but was forced on them by the presence of an increasingly-organized proletariat. Classes, forms of power, and the nature of the state have to be considered in relational terms, not in terms of pure opposition and confrontation. If the latter conception is adopted, then the resultant form of politics is one of 'substitution' or 'replacement'; the convenient Marxist formula which substitutes 'real' or 'direct' democracy for 'formal' democracy: a politics of dual power which effectively squeezes out the necessity for the political transformation of those other areas where democracy may be inscribed – the hegemonic apparatuses of the bourgeois representative state which is constituted elsewhere than at the level of the capital/labour contradiction.[9] In this context, democracy cannot be considered as necessarily 'attached' to a particular form of government (political society) but must be analysed in the complex processes of its articulation to the bourgeois 'integral state', (political society *plus* civil society). Democracy is a historically-negotiated concept.

In his critique of Hegel and other bourgeois theorists who attempted to establish a 'natural' relation between democracy and the various forms of bourgeois state which they attempted to justify, Marx was aware that democracy had no fixed meaning. He was to give democracy a class definition and connotation and a specific historical variability. As with his analysis of the state, the primary focus was on its *class* character, established as a criterion for the critique of the Hegelian conception of the state and philosophy of law.

If we accept that Marx's work is complete and a coherent body of theory then there is no problem: all democracy is class democracy, it is assigned a necessary class-belonging and its possible connotation with other determinants is excluded. But if, as recent work by Marxists has shown, there are radical discontinuities and breaks in the development of Marx's work and if, for example, it can be shown that the analysis of the state in Marx and Engels is partial and incomplete, then it is also possible to argue that the related conception of democracy also lacks a consistent theorization.[10]

These are not just pedantic questions since it is not just Marx's text we are concerned with but its effects on a whole political and theoretical tradition and on one very important aspect in particular: the theory and political practice of *transition*. Between the economic and class reductionism of the Second International, resurrected in the Third, the theory of transition, along with the theory of ideology and of the state as a complex form, was effectively excluded. Accepting the absolute primacy of the 'economic base' this tradition has had no problem with these latter areas since it considered that a transformation of production relations necessarily resulted in transformations elsewhere. Since democracy only has a class connotation, a transformation in class relations automatically gives it a new meaning; no transition, just substitution. Economy and politics collapse into a model of mutual and necessary correspondence, as though the critique of political economy in Marx was a simple critique of the political 'in' the economic or the economic 'in' the political.

Against this conception it may be necessary to pose, as Gramsci did in 1917, a 'Revolution against *Capital*' in the sense that *Capital* is not just the book but also the interpretation of it by the theorists of the Second International; an interpretation which, as Gramsci argued, found its living contradiction in the experience of the October Revolution.[11] Gramsci's own work, as I will argue below, provides the basis for a theory of transition in his conceptions of the integral state, the specificity of the political, passive revolution and hegemony as *index* of democratic transition in the bourgeois representative democracies. For the present it is enough to register his 'Revolution against *Capital*' to suggest a complex and largely untheorized space between the analysis of the mode of production and the representative state: a space in which the concept of democracy is a prime issue.

In this light we can continue with the examination of the multiple definitions of democracy. The tendency within the Marxist tradition to assign democracy to a necessary class-belonging is in many ways complicit with the liberal state's own conception of it. By 'naturalizing' and neutralizing it and making it appear as an integral element of its construction from the beginning, democracy has been made to appear as inseparable from a certain form of government and economic system. One of the aspects central to the formation and stability of any ideological system is the establishment of what Michel Foucault calls 'continuous histories'[12] or 'traditions' which can look back to justify their existence. But these traditions of course are far from being 'natural'; they are constructed, materialized over a long historical process of negotiation.

The historical fact is that democracy cannot be said to 'belong' to the liberal state but was articulated to it at quite a late stage in its development in order to carry out, as it were, Hobbes's advice that a notion of representation is central to the formation of a 'sturdy' civil society; and nowhere is this sturdier than in Britain where the articulation of democracy is possibly more diffuse and complex than in any other state. But again this is not the only available context of democracy. In the socialist countries it is genuinely related, through one of its many connotations, to a certain levelling-out of social and economic rights. It is at that level, perfectly justifiable within the Marxist tradition, rather than at the level of the state or representation that its dominant meaning operates in such countries. In the countries of the Third World democracy takes on yet another meaning: a connotation which is neither defined in purely class terms nor in terms of liberal parliamentary representation, but in terms of the 'people' – a *national* connotation which predominates in countries where 'pure' class struggle was not first on the agenda but the overthrow of foreign imperialist powers.

Three sets of connotations derived variously from Hobbes and Locke, Rousseau, and Marx, can be identified which suggest a complexity which denies the possibility of collapsing the word and the reality of democracy into any one of its possible meanings – its representative form, its popular form or its class form. It must in effect embrace all of these. There is no pure 'bourgeois' democracy which can be posed as simply opposite to 'proletarian' democracy or replaced by it in a revolutionary *fiat*. The articulation of these meanings of democracy is central to the development of a concept of transition in Marxist theory and practice which would reject the simple dichotomy of 'formal' and 'direct' democracy and its associated strategic models.

IV. LUXEMBURG'S CRITIQUE

It was Rosa Luxemburg who provided the first Marxist critique of Lenin and Trotsky from the point of view of democracy. Aware of the complexity of its meaning and articulation she criticized Kautsky, Lenin and Trotsky for simple equations and oppositions:

The basic error of the Lenin–Trotsky theory is that they too, just like Kautsky, oppose dictatorship to democracy. 'Dictatorship *or* democracy' is the way the question is put by Bolsheviks and Kautsky alike. The latter naturally decides in favour of 'democracy', that is, of bourgeois democracy, precisely because he opposes it to the alternative of the socialist revolution. Lenin and Trotsky, on the other hand, decide in favour of dictatorship in contradistinction to democracy, and thereby, in favour of the dictatorship of a handful of persons, that is, in favour of dictatorship on the bourgeois model. They are two opposite poles, both alike being far removed from a genuine socialist policy.[13]

And to Trotsky's assertion that 'We have never been (as Marxists) idol-worshippers of formal democracy', Luxemburg replies:

All that really means is: We have always distinguished the social kernel from the political form of *bourgeois* democracy; we have always revealed the hard kernel of social inequality and lack of freedom hidden under the sweet shell of formal equality and freedom – not in order to reject the latter but to spur the working class into not being satisfied with the shell, but rather, by conquering political power, to create a socialist democracy to replace bourgeois democracy – not to eliminate democracy altogether.[14]

The metaphors of shell and kernel, form and content, were ultimately to confine Luxemburg herself to the limits of the violence/legality dichotomy precisely by their inability to come to terms with the *relational* nature of state power and the necessary periodization of political transition, but none the less her critique indicates some of the complexities involved.

This critique was directed primarily to the dismissal by Lenin and Trotsky of the Constituent Assembly, of universal suffrage and of the freedom of press and assembly, and to the emergence of a one-party government after the Brest-Litovsk Treaty with Germany in 1918. The argument for the 'special conditions' of War Communism inevitably arises at this point: the difficulties of the besieged young socialist state surrounded by hostile forces. But I believe that it is possible to suggest that the arguments used by Lenin, and more especially by Trotsky, are more than just pragmatic or conjunctural adaptations of a 'pure' theory to a particularly difficult situation. It should be argued, I think, that in many ways, the outcome to this situation was already implicit in the theory itself precisely because of a characteristic conflation of the economic and political moments which I will discuss below. In effect this means that Marxism does not retain its integrity simply to be moulded to different historical situations; the absence of a fully theorized conception of democracy was, and still is, one of its major absences.

Trotsky was especially guilty of a particular inverted form of 'parliamentary cretinism', in Luxemburg's view. His reliance on empirical parliamentary data to argue his case that although there had been a leftward shift by the population towards the Bolsheviks and Social Revolutionaries, three-quarters of the candidates for the new Assembly were 'right wing' and his assertion that the Constituent Assembly reflects once and for all 'the mental composition, political maturity and mood of its electorate just at the moment when the latter goes to the polls'[15] is a simple mirror image of the liberal *total* reliance on elections; a *total* mistrust. In addition to this, both Lenin and Trotsky argued that the Assembly was a 'cumbersome mechanism'. By accepting the Assembly's own image of itself as the 'head' of the representative body or as a pure emanation of the bourgeoisie, a formal device, Lenin and Trotsky implicitly ignored the contradictions already implicit in the very existence of the Assembly. Contradictions which were already constituted through forms of class conflict prior to the October Revolution: the presence in some form, however inadequate, of the people *within* the state – a presence which was already tracing a possible connotation for democracy since the representative form itself could not be immediately identified with the autocratic state. As well as being a 'palliative', the Constituent Assembly was also a necessary concession forced by the presence of class struggle. It was not a 'screen' for the state but an internal contradiction.

It is still possible of course to argue for Lenin and Trotsky from the point of view of expediency and national imperatives. But we cannot ignore that what was then conjunctural became inexorably organic and permanent within the political and state structure of the Soviet Union with Lenin's death and the ascendancy of Stalin. He, it must be said, did not act 'cynically' in a lust for power, but justified his actions from the available body of Marxist theory, marked as it was by economic and class reductionism in which a concept of political transition is sacrificed in favour of a politics of substitution and replacement. Party becomes state, state becomes party. State as 'instrument' of the bourgeoisie becomes state as 'instrument' of the proletariat, and what disappears in the equation is precisely any political appropriation of a democratic terrain which might have been constituted at a distance from either state or class, and which might not have been covered by the then existing definitions of the political. This was a terrain which could not have been recognized by a politics which recognizes only the 'terminal' forms of political power – the state, the Assembly, etc.; it was a terrain which had to wait for the concept of *hegemony* in Gramsci's formulations to reveal its full extent as a complex and dispersed matrix of power relations.

Clearly then, the problems arising from this revolutionary moment are not reducible to errors of judgement. The implications were already there in (i) a certain conception of the state and (ii) a certain conception of politics: two conceptions which provide the theoretical basis for the notion of *dual power*. In a frontal attack on that object or 'monolith' designated the state which is where power is located, power is 'seized' and an *anti-state*, the Soviets, is substituted for it. Central to this conception of strategy is the belief that the state is an 'object' or 'machine' to be removed, that power is a quantifiable substance to be seized and held, and that the institutions of representative democracy can justifiably be replaced since they are only the 'emanations' of a class – the bourgeoisie. From this comes the formula: representative democracy = bourgeois democracy = bourgeois dictatorship, in a multiple and reductive conflation of politics, economics and ideology. For Lenin and Trotsky the representative state is simply the evidence of the class and economic power of the bourgeoisie, and is therefore reducible to a form of economic organization to be replaced by another form, the Soviets. For Kautsky on the other hand, the representative state has nothing to do with economics, being purely a 'voluntaristic construct' of the 'will of the bourgeoisie' in a complete autonomy of politics, economics and ideology. Either complete conflation or complete separation; permutations already implicit in a certain conception of base and superstructure.

Similar issues were at stake in the debate between Lenin and Trotsky on the trade unions in 1920–1, where Trotsky was to argue that the workers would not need trade unions to protect themselves against their own workers' state since their interests converged. Lenin, on the other hand, argued for the independence of the unions from the state precisely because, although the unions and the state *represent* the working class, the state was subject to 'bureaucratic distortions' which the workers should be able to defend themselves from. Lenin's recognition of the contradictions inherent in specifically different forms of representation (economic and political) is incisive here: a resistance to the conflation that Trotsky was trying to effect in his programme for the 'militarization of labour' and which Gramsci was later to condemn as a form of 'Bonapartism'.[16]

So from this moment in the history of the communist movement there arise a number of political and theoretical options whose related effects are multiple and self-reproducing. The evacuation of any space between politics and economics means that any notion of process or of transition, of a multiple and differentiated struggle, first of all to recognize and then to confront the network of power relations *between* the terminal forms of power (the network which characterizes the hegemony and not just the domination of the bourgeoisie) – the struggle for the creation of new forms of democracy – is excluded. This, as I have said, depends upon a conception of the state as an 'instrument' or object to be seized, manipulated or simply smashed. Related to this is the identification of power as a quantifiable substance to be grasped from its original location in the hands of another class and brought over to our side. History becomes a question of pure domination. The logic is inexorable; ideology becomes 'false consciousness', politics becomes manipulation or revelation and so on. But this logic has been challenged in recent years by developments in Marxist theory; a challenge which, I would argue, is already implicit in Gramsci's work, and it is through three concepts from his work – the integral state, consent, and passive revolution – that I now

114   COLIN MERCER

want to examine the question of democracy between the disabling
alternatives of Revolution and Reform.

V. THE INTEGRAL STATE:

(a) Gramsci and Lenin

Due partly to the difficult conditions under which he wrote the *Prison Notebooks* but largely to a genuinely open-ended and interrogative style, Gramsci's formulations on the state, as on his other major concepts, are not systematically expounded. They are partial, fragmentary and sometimes frustrating in their schematic nature. But none the less in their conjunctural applications and in their insistence on 'reconnoitring the terrain' from many angles, these formulations are enabling rather than simply prescriptive. His most famous formulation on the state is concerned with the differences between the Eastern state and the Western:

In Russia the state was everything, civil society was primordial and gelatinous; in the West, there was a proper relation between state and civil society, and when the state trembled a sturdy structure of civil society was at once revealed. The state was only an outer ditch, behind which there stood a powerful system of fortresses and earthworks: more or less numerous from one state to the next, it goes without saying – but this precisely necessitated an accurate reconnaissance of each individual country.[17]

The perspective is comparative, the metaphors spatial and military, but this formulation none the less contains Gramsci's insistence on the necessity to understand that the state must be theorized always in relation to civil society and not as a single and abstract moment of represssion or force. The identification of the state simply with government is a confusion of civil society with political society and a representation purely of the economic-corporate moment of a given social formation. In order to understand the *hegemony* of a particular group the methodology has to be extended:

For it should be remarked that the general notion of state includes elements which need to be referred back to the notion of civil society (in the sense that one might say that state = political society + civil society, in other words, hegemony protected by the armour of coercion).[18]

And it is necessary to add here, as against Perry Anderson, that civil society is not understood by Gramsci as 'external' to the state, that it is not 'equivalent' to parliamentary democracy in the West which, when threatened, reveals the same *essential* and repressive core as the state in the East. Gramsci in fact moves away from the purely spatial and military conception of the relation between state and civil society quoted above, first of all by insisting that the distinction is *methodological* and not organic, and then by theorizing the integral state in the following terms as, '. . . the entire complex of practical and theoretical activities with which the ruling class not only justifies and maintains its dominance, but manages to win the active consent of those over whom it rules'.[19]

This represents more than the 'addition' of dominant ideas and attitudes to a given economic base and its 'executive committee', the state; it suggests a decisive reformulation of the conception of the state away from a simple notion of representation and away from instrumentalist conceptions, towards what Nicos Poulantzas has called a 'relational theory of state power'[20] which is not primarily concerned with the 'institutions' of domination as particular 'objects' to which ideology is 'added' and in which power is simply located at centres to be attacked.

With these partial formulations in mind we can now return to Lenin. Lenin's great achievement was to recognize the specificity of the political, the concentrated centre of its operations within the Russian state. In theorizing this specificity he argued that 'trade union consciousness' was not enough and that there had to be a certain element introduced from 'outside': the revolutionary party as a vanguard of professional revolutionaries. Strategically and conjuncturally this seems to have been a correct manoeuvre but problems arise precisely in the definition of what is 'inside' and what is 'outside', and these definitions in turn will depend upon a certain conception of 'structure' – what it includes and what it excludes, and then whether these definitions remain constant as the struggle develops. Clearly the structure with which Lenin was most concerned was that of the state, but in fact his own formulations and propositions on this particular structure underwent various transformations from the end of the nineteenth century to *The State and Revolution* in 1917 and between the latter text and *The Proletarian Revolution and the Renegade Kautsky* in 1918, when the construction of a new socialist state was the priority. Clearly Lenin was himself aware that the Marxist theory of the state was an open theory being forged in confrontation, and his focus on its repressive aspects represents only one moment in its development, something which Lenin was aware of when he defined it as a 'special' machine.

To meet the state of the bourgeoisie, Lenin formulated the 'anti-state' of the working class embodied in the revolutionary party. This took the form of a response to the centralization of the political where the political is conceived of as the moment of force or repression: the life of the masses as directly political domination, or pure subjection to a state to which they had a relation of exteriority embodied in the edifice of the Winter Palace. As a response to this particular structure, the anti-state is adequate. But clearly the anti-state depends upon what conception of the state you have in the first place.

It is at this point that two important questions have to be posed. First, was Lenin's definition of the state adequate on its own terms or does it, as Lenin himself hinted, represent only one moment of that process of definition? Second, are we now confronted with the same form of state if we do accept that Lenin's definition was adequate? If we accept the adequacy of Lenin's definition, it simply becomes a question for us of retaining the theoretical propositions and simply adjusting tactics to a new 'concrete situation', but if we are not completely satisfied with Lenin's formulations, if we do not accept them as a complete theory of the state, a double problem arises. First, historical – the vastly different historical conjuncture in which we find ourselves, today, second, theoretical – the extension of the theory of the state beyond the definition of its concentrated political functions and repressive aspects.

It is crucial for democratic strategy today that we consider just how 'special' this 'machine' is by going beyond the 'economic-corporate' definition of the state which confines it purely to the realm of political government. Gramsci's 'integral state' can enable us to approach the two aspects of this problem, theoretical and historical.

Much of the debate on Gramsci's work and on its implications for revolutionary strategy has taken as its central motif the famous metaphor, quoted above, where the state in Russia is compared to the state in the West. If we leave it at that, what emerges is a general picture which suggests that Lenin was adequate for the East and Gramsci for the West, or that Gramsci was the 'Lenin' of the Italian situation, as Togliatti proposed. This is a tempting picture, but I would argue that the truth is rather more complex and that this picture, with its historical and comparative emphasis, tends to exclude some of the key theoretical issues at stake: Gramsci becomes simply another figure in the continuous

Marxist tradition who added something more to it but did not challenge any of its basic principles.

Against this 'continuous history' I would argue that precisely because Gramsci develops his major concepts from the starting-point of an historical analysis of the formation and development of bourgeois states (England, France, Italy) and their specific configurations of hegemony, *and* combines these analyses with theoretical propositions on the nature of revolutionary strategy 'now', he is the first Marxist to attempt the articulation of a strategy for the process of the formation of the new society ('historical bloc') with an analysis of the modalities of this process based on the actually existing complex relation for forces. It is in this context, in his *Prison Notebooks* at least, that his conception of the complex forms of representation in the bourgeois democratic states, enables him to resist any simple substitution of 'direct' for 'formal' democracy.[21] Against the historicist reduction of Gramsci to 'theorist of the revolution in the West' or the 'Italian Lenin', it must be emphasized that his writings go beyond a particular and local reference and contain a challenge to certain dominant forms of Marxist discourse.

(b) The revaluation of civil society

Gramsci's 'integral state' represents an advance on the Leninist analysis of the moment of 'force' by giving a more adequate theoretical weighting to the moment of 'consent'. The theory of the 'integral state' leads to a revaluation of civil society as a domain with its own specific autonomies and effects. Developed by Gramsci out of the ambiguities in Marx's own work and with more than a slight debt to Hegel, the concept of civil society in Gramsci challenges the monolith of history and domination implicit in much Marxist discourse – a monolith which is one-dimensional and spatial, reinforced by the 'edifice' of base and superstructure and allocating certain spaces to the economic and the political. In spite of the famous metaphor of 'trenches' and 'fortifications' in his comparison of the state in the East and the West, the major direction of Gramsci's work is away from the conception in which the state is *essential* and given, and civil society acts as an illusory 'front'. These two moments for Gramsci cannot be understood in terms of cause and effect, essence and phenomenom. Like base and superstructure, which Gramsci rarely uses in isolation, their varying threshold of separation and proximity will depend on the relative equilibrium of economic, political and ideological forces.

The distinction between state and civil society is, for Gramsci 'methodological and not organic'[22] and the terms of their definition are therefore *conjunctural* and not *a priori*. From this point of view he is able to analyse the specific weaknesses of Italian civil society and hegemony precisely because of its 'unsuccessful' or passive bourgeois revolution – the *Risorgimento* and its inability to forge a unity between the newly-ascendant bourgeoisie and the popular masses in terms of *active consent*. This was a weakness which was to lead to the crisis of the Italian liberal state in the first part of this century; a weakness which was to result in Mussolini's 'strong state' which was not simply the result of the intervention of finance or large capital but rather the outcome of the conquest of civil society by occupying the ideological terrains of identity, authority and representation; terrains which were vacated by an economistic Marxism. Other states had specifically different responses to similar crises; Roosevelt's New Deal in the USA or the dispersal of immediate forms of confrontation by the complex nature of bourgeois hegemony in Britain with its mass Labour Party and the emergence of the Welfare State.

It is in the revaluation of civil society, proceeding from an historical analysis of its formation, that ideological struggle comes to take its place within democratic struggle. Civil society is not expressive of the state, nor does it have to answer to it since it has its own forms of autonomy which open up contradictions between itself and the state in the narrow sense of 'political society'. And from this historical analysis of its importance in the formation of bourgeois hegemony arise the implications for democratic strategy. If the relative equilibrium between state and civil society is disturbed, as has been increasingly the case in the West since the beginning of the 1930s, areas which had previously been considered as 'non-political' or outside the sphere of the political in the narrow sense become politicized. This disturbance has become particularly intense since the nineteen-sixties with the politicization of the 'personal' represented by the Women's Movement or with the politicization of the environment by ecology movements and many other forms of struggle, regional and specific, which could not be categorized under the heading of 'class'.

Any strategy which fails to understand the state in the integral sense as the moment of hegemony as well as the moment of domination, and which ignores the historical and uneven nature of those 'private organisms' *designated* civil society by concentrating on the narrowly political moment of force, will trample in its path any dispersed representative forms and democratic liberties constituted at that level. It will not necessarily do this wilfully: it will trample them underfoot since it could not have recognized that they were there while looking for the 'downward' movement of repression or pure domination. Firstly a recognition of the historical existence of civil society in the formation of bourgeois states, and secondly a theorization of the materiality of its existence now would seem to me to be absolutely crucial for any democratic strategy today in so far as it allows a space for new political forms of transition to emerge.

By interpreting history as a monolithic process of 'downward' movement with no relational 'upward' movement from the dispersed and differentially subjected agents which 'live' in civil society, representative democracy comes to be understood as simply an 'imposed' form and therefore purely formal. If civil society is revalued, in Gramsci's terms, as a site of multiple 'representations' necessary for the maintenance of a complex and diffuse hegemony, and not simply as the 'vertical' form of representation characteristic of parliamentary democracy, then the question of a democratic struggle becomes not one of replacement but of the articulation of diverse and regional forms of struggle with the struggle to transform the 'separation of powers' built into the current bourgeois representative structure. In this sense the revaluation of civil society and the recognition of new terrains for struggle which is central to the concept of hegemony, at once recognizes the state in its integral form and becomes an anti-statist principle, providing the criteria for its transformation.

Furthermore, the revaluation of civil society, designating the complex and differentiated moment of active consent, stresses the *relational* nature of state power. Classes, defined at the level of the capital-labour contradiction, do not simply confront each other for battle in an open space in a battle for a single object – the state or power. The forms of the contradiction are *already present* in the very form of the state. The state, in its integral sense, is constituted, condensed, materialized, through a complex and historically and nationally variable interplay of economic, political and ideological forces which for Gramsci makes up the 'historic bloc': a yoking together of heterogeneous elements in a relatively stable equilibrium which Gramsci characterizes as a 'contradictory and discordant ensemble'.[23]

The historical bloc is in this sense by no means equivalent to the concept of a 'power bloc' which embodies only the moment of coercion. This historic bloc, by including active consent, resists the notion that power can be said to 'belong' here or there, with this or that class. The state is not a pre-existing essence but a complex and variable configuration of forces and points of resistance. It is in this sense that Poulantzas argues that not only is there no Marxist theory of the state, but that there cannot be a general theory of the state in Marxism. No *a priori* judgements can be brought to the analysis of any state either in terms of the logic of capital, or the necessary coherence of ideology, or of international capital, etc. Like culture, language, national histories and boundaries, which are all crucial elements in the hegemony of national states, the state itself is a strategic field which has to be examined in its complex processes of construction and formation in order to understand *this* specific configuration of hegemony.

(c) New terrains for struggle

This focus on conjunctural analysis, the 'reconnaissance of each individual terrain' in Gramsci, the avoidance of general models, involves a necessary regionalization and democratization of theory as a necessary precondition for formulating a complex and diffuse democratic strategy – a strategy which would be able to embrace, for example, national particularities without the evacuation of politics embodied in many calls for 'proletarian internationalism'. It could also provide a theoretical and strategic basis, and not just an opportunistic one, for the coordination of those struggles which have been asymmetrical to class struggle, such as those around sexuality (the democratization of the body itself),[24] or in relations between men and women, or in the educational apparatuses, regional planning, neighbourhood councils and so on – the dispersed forms of economic, political and ideological hegemony which can only be recognized and granted their own forms of autonomy if the conception of the monolithic state is shattered.

This has begun to happen: its first stage was the recognition that the state was traversed by contradictions and conflicts within the ruling bloc itself (between small and big capital); this was the stage, in terms of communist politics, of the 'anti-monopoly alliance'. But this conception still recognizes the state as the moment of simple domination (state monopoly capitalism). The second stage is in the acknowledgement that the contradictions of the state are not only a question of conflicting interests within the ruling bloc, but also between them and the dominated classes. The history of states and of their specific contemporary forms, is always also a history which is traced by popular struggles of varying degrees of intensity, which have negotiated a presence within the state itself. Historically this is particularly the case since the thirties, but it is also a *theoretical* reality since the emergence of any hegemony always requires that presence to secure an active consent to its existence.

The historical presence of the masses *within* the integral state is not an argument for a social-democratic strategy of 'management' and piecemeal transformation of already-existing structures, since the process of negotiation which has forced this presence has not been a confrontation of equal forces: it is a *loaded* negotiation since the masses are not there on their own terms. Whilst being 'present' by virtue of their own struggles and the winning of certain concessions, and whilst the variable relation of forces will affect the form of the state, the existence of these forces is not, as Poulantzas emphasizes, in terms of their own apparatuses, since the dominant class is active too in the perpetual reconstitution of its own unity – a constant process of keeping the subordinate classes at the corporate level, preventing the possibility of any autonomy for them within *this* state. This is precisely what the concept of hegemony designates; that active consent is not 'imposed' but negotiated by unequal forces in a complex and uneven confrontation of downward and upward movement in which a series of relatively stable compromises establishes a contradictory equilibrium. This was the motif which Gramsci saw in Machiavelli's famous 'centaur'; a paradoxical and contradictory unity of force and consent, dictatorship and democracy, which he updates for the 'Modern Prince' by preventing it from becoming a simple dichotomy of violence/legality, through his theorization of the integral state and the formation of hegemony.[25]

The concept of the integral state as the hegemonic moment articulating diverse elements into a relative unity resists the establishment of any necessary correspondences between, for example, democracy and the representative state, capitalism and representative democracy or, what is more important for us, between socialism and democracy. These are all correspondences which are not given or fixed, but have to be constructed in the formation of any historic bloc. This construction, as the emergence of the bourgeois representative state in Britain has shown over the three hundred years of its formation,[26] is a complex and diffuse process involving the negotiation of multiple factors, not just economic but also political, ideological, cultural, philosophical, linguistic, spatial and sexual; all domains to which democratic strategy must extend. It is with respect to these domains that Michel Foucault's work is relevant to the formulation of a democratic strategy.

(d) Foucault, knowledge and power

Foucault's work is concerned with the relation of knowledge to power, with the historical emergence of 'disciplines' – natural science, grammar, theory of wealth, and the related areas of medicine, law, psychiatry. This field of interest may not appear to have any relevance for a consideration of democracy except that Foucault is explicitly not concerned simply with a 'history of ideas' but with the concrete processes of their dispersal and sedimentation in ideology. In a similar way to Gramsci's formulations on the relations between 'common sense' and philosophy which establish the 'intellectual and moral leadership' necessary for any hegemony,[27] Foucault examines the couplet knowledge/power and the material forms of its existence and effects in the bourgeois states. Resisting the separation of 'ideas' and 'practice', Foucault uses the concept of 'discourse' in his analysis of the nature of power. Discourse, Foucault states, is where power and knowledge are joined together:

Discourses are tactical elements or blocks operating in the field of force relations: there can exist different and even contradictory discourses within the same strategy: they can, on the contrary, circulate without changing their form from one strategy to another, opposing strategy.[28]

The first proposition we can derive from this is that discourse does not mean 'ideas'; it designates rather the historical forms of their materialization and diffusion as ideology which for Gramsci also was not a 'system of ideas' (criticizing Bukharin), but an 'epistemological and structural matter.'

Ideology is not a question of 'beliefs' or of being 'true' or 'false' consciousness, but is to be analysed in terms of its historical *effectivity* and *materiality*. Ideology does not 'belong' to this or that class but is constructed and negotiated through a complex network of force relations. From this we can derive a second proposition; that discourses, as the junction of power and knowledge, are not reducible to the operations of particular (class) agents or (class) subjects and that therefore the whole conception, implicit in much of the Marxist tradition that power is a quantifiable 'substance' to be seized or located in particular institutions (terminal forms) is problematized. Power, Foucault argues, is not to be located in a central point, a unique source of sovereignty:

Power is not an institution, and not a structure; neither is it a certain strength we are endowed with; it is the name one attributes to a complex strategical situation in a particular society . . . Power is not something that is acquired, seized or shared . . . Power is exercised from innumerable points, in the interplay of nonegalitarian and mobile relations.

And Foucault goes on to stress

the strictly relational character of power relationships. Their existence depends on a multiplicity of points of resistance . . . where there is power there is resistance, and yet, or rather consequently, this resistance is never in a position of exteriority in relation to power.[29]

Implicit in these formulations is a critique of those forms of analysis, Marxist and otherwise, which reduce the question of power to an 'effect of obedience':

Theories of government and the traditional analyses of their mechanisms certainly don't exhaust the field where power is exercised and where it functions.

And more explicitly in relation to Marxism, he adds:

We now know with reasonable certainty who receives the profits, which people are involved, and we know how these funds are reinvested. But as for power. . . . We know that it is not in the hands of those who govern. But, of course, the idea of the 'ruling class' has never received an adequate formulation, and neither have other terms, such as 'to dominate', 'to rule', 'to govern', etc.[30]

Foucault said this in 1972, and the fact that in his more recent work, *The History of Sexuality* (1976), he uses the concept of hegemony (or 'hegemonies'), suggests that perhaps there was an earlier, more adequate formulation of the idea of the 'ruling class' in the work of Gramsci. In fact, I would argue that this *relational* theory of power exists, 'in the practical state' in Gramsci's formulations on the integral state and the nature of hegemony. At this intersection of Foucault and Gramsci, a radically new strategic perspective emerges which Foucault voiced in the following terms:

It is possible that the struggles now taking place and the local, regional and discontinuous theories that derive from these struggles and that are indissociable from them stand at the threshold of our discovery of the manner in which power is exercised.[31]

A necessary regionalization and democratization of theory and strategy, and the coordination of points of resistance to meet the multiple relations of power and their diffusion which characterize hegemony, becomes a prerequisite for any democratic strategy – a conception which displaces the Left/Right, Maximalist/Reformist options which dispute whether hegemony is established 'before' or 'after' the seizure of power.

To summarize on the integral state: the state is not an 'object' or 'essence' and is not reducible to a set of institutions. The integral state requires a revaluation of civil society as methodologically inseparable from it but subject to varying relations of forces. The integration of civil society and state represents the hegemonic moment when a relatively stable, though contradictory, unity is established and able to reproduce itself. This production is effected not from 'above' but in the proliferation of discourses which secure *active consent*. Power simultaneously has to be conceived as an unequal interaction of forces and resistances; *force and consent*.

An analysis of power using the concept of the integral state cannot simply be based on the 'terminal forms' of the economic and the political but also has to embrace the 'middle ground' of mobile relations and processes which are not reducible to 'effects' of an economic cause. The integral state resists the conception of history as a monolithic process of subjection and subordination of the 'masses' and suggests a revaluation of that latter concept itself, which I will approach in the next section. Strategically, the concept of the integral state, resists spatial and military metaphors and moves beyond the pervasive discourse of Revolution and Reform to designate a new terrain for democratic struggle which could embrace a concept of periodization and transition by articulating the transformation of the 'vertical' forms of parliamentary representation with the creation of new *means* of representation, between 'parliamentary cretinism' on the one hand, and 'council cretinism' (dual power) on the other. By allowing a space between class interests and general interests, this strategy could come to terms with power relations constituted on terrains which Marxism on the whole has not been able to recognize. That we are all *in* this enlarged conception of the state is the necessary starting point for democratic and revolutionary strategy.

VI. CONSENT

Precisely how 'concrete individuals' are present within the integral state is a question of some importance for the problem of democracy. This is a question we can approach from the Gramscian concept of consent or, more correctly, *active consent*. The integral state, as the ensemble of practical and theoretical activities by which the ruling class secures active consent requires an 'actor' (a subject) who 'consents'. Central to Gramsci's formulations on the emergence of bourgeois hegemony is the notion that this 'concrete individual' is never a pre-given entity or an essential human subject. Man, Gramsci writes, should be conceived of 'as a series of active relationships (a process) in which individuality, though perhaps the most important, is not however the only element to be taken into account'.[32] Or elsewhere:

Man is to be conceived as an historical bloc of purely individual and subjective elements and of mass and objective or material elements with which the individual is in an active relationship.[33]

And he adds that it is not enough to know these active relationships as they exist at any given moment of time; 'they must be known genetically in the movement of their formation'.[34]

For Gramsci, this 'movement of their formation' is precisely the movement of the formation of the integral state which requires for its existence not just 'masses', which are somehow external to it, but complex ideological subjects constituted internally to the power relations which maintain it. In this sense the Gramscian concept of consent has a dual critical status. First, against the tradition of bourgeois political theory from Locke to the present day, consent for Gramsci is not a general and pregiven category. It is implicitly accompanied by the question; who consents, and to what? There is no consent in general; hegemony is specifically variable according to classes and historical periods. Second, in relation to the Marxist tradition, the Gramscian concept of consent represents a shift away from the militarized Leninist discourse of the 'war of manoeuvre' of 'masses', towards a conception which could embrace differentially-subjected ideological subjects positioned not only as masses but also as 'men', 'women', 'intellectuals', 'professionals', 'national minorities' and so on. In the same direction, consent also designates a complex and non-monolithic conception of ideology which is not conceived as 'false consciousness' or a unified 'world-view'. In the complex structure of the historic bloc – 'the discordant ensemble' – ideology does not belong to, or emanate from, particular classes but is constructed at the intersection of these multiple subject positions which, though *overdetermined* by class struggle, cannot be said to be directly determined by it or reducible to its effects.

These formulations can be expanded if we refer again to Foucault's suggestion that the history of bourgeois states is not simply one of repression, but also of the 'proliferation of discourses'. To this we should add that discourses have as their unifying principle, an ideological subject which is constituted internally to this discourse. The most obvious example of this is the emergence of a particular juridical, free, ethical subject with the establishment of the bourgeois juridical apparatus, but at a more pervasive level this subject in turn interacts with a certain type of familial subject, sexual subject (male subject, female subject), racial subject, aesthetic subject and so on. For hegemony to be established, these varying, and possibly contradictory, subject positions have to be maintained in a relative unity. The function of ideology is the production and maintenance of these subject positions: ideology 'interpellates' (names, hails, places) individuals as subjects in such a way as to make individuals recognize themselves and identity themselves not as constructed, determinate, but as given and determinant.[35]

The proliferation of discourses; on education, natural philosophy, political economy, law, theories of wealth, grammar, national languages, conceptions (in medicine) of the body, the categorizations of madness and sanity, the structure of the family, the role of women and so on, are not just episodes in a history of ideas, but have the very real effect of positioning certain subjects who can know, write, act, accuse, control, etc. And these various subjects have to be held together in a connotative system where each interpellated subject evokes others – most obviously the familial subject evoking a particular form of sexual subject and so on.

It was with the emergence of the bourgeois integral state that the need to create these subjects and yoke them together in a relative unity first arose to meet the needs of increased forms of social organization and an expanding civil society where simple 'vertical' representations (individual-householder-state) were not enough and where multiple representations and recognitions had to be established from all directions in a relation of *connotation*. The integral state, to secure active and 'spontaneous' consent, requires this complex network of ideological subjects constituted at the intersection of multiple discourses. This is not a question of ideas being 'imposed' from above on pregiven individuals, but of the complex forms of the construction (interpellation) of those 'concrete individuals' as subjects. Discourses position their subjects in their subjectivity itself. Foucault argues that even the biological body is not a given but a *construct* which varies historically and that a certain understanding of the body (and the corollaries of control, inspection, and potential for action) was also involved in the formation of the bourgeois State:

The emphasis on the body should undoubtedly be linked to the process of growth and establishment of bourgeois hegemony; not, however, because of the market value assumed by labour capacity, but because of what the 'cultivation' of its own body could represent politically, economically and historically for the present and future of the bourgeoisie.[36]

This is an insight which, at another level, the Women's Movement has engaged with today, and one which suggests that the question of democracy cannot be confined to external political options in the narrow sense.

From these formulations it is possible to argue that democracy within the representative state has not simply been a question of the 'head' or of the 'will' and that it could therefore be 'revealed', from another class position, to be purely illusory or formal. Democracy in fact has been profoundly inscribed within a certain conception of the human individual as a complex ideological subject where the related categories of 'sovereignty', 'choice', 'ownership', 'consciousness', 'soul' and 'freedom' all play their part in an 'economy' of self-assuring representations which are not reducible to effects of the narrowly political and governmental apparatus (political society). The revaluation of civil society as the site of that 'economy' of representations and their role in producing active consent designates new terrains with which a democratic strategy should engage. This recognition is implicit in Gramsci's work and provides us with a critique of the militarized discourse of masses and confrontation which reaches its ultimate peak in Trotsky. This is not to say that the need for a conception of masses and confrontation disappears but simply that its discourse which delimits a certain number of prescriptions, choices, options and alternatives is displaced. It is a curious paradox that in this process of displacement Gramsci himself had to resort to the military metaphor of the 'war of position' to theorize these new sites of struggle and a conception of the party which goes beyond simple vanguardism.

In Britain especially we have to consider the extremely complex configurations of consent over a long historical period. The trajectory which leads from Hobbes and Locke in the seventeenth century in a process of sedimentation and dispersal through the nineteenth-century ideologies of utilitarianism and self-help, to the common-sense sub-stratum of enterprise, initiative and the self-made man of Thatcherist discourse today, is an eloquent and effective testimony to Gramsci's formulations on the relation between philosophy and common sense and the role of the intellectuals in the establishment, or, more correctly, negotiation, of hegemony[37] – a hegemony in this case where the complex meaning of democracy is probably more pervasive than in any other country.

This process was not a political 'con-trick' but essential to the process of 'individuation' which Poulantzas describes as an integral element in the formation of the bourgeois representative nation state.[38] It is a crucial paradox to be recognized by any democratic strategy in Britain today that the British state, uniquely without a *written* constitution, should have been able to *inscribe* the notion of democracy so deeply within its structure and its subjects. A certain conception of democracy is so deeply embedded within common-sense attitudes, and reinforced from all directions, so closely and effectively articulated to the bourgeois representative state, that it is more than a narrowly political task to *disarticulate* its meanings for a strategy of transition. An analysis of the specific forms of the configuration of consent and of the various modes of inscription of hegemony which would take us beyond the empirically-observable 'edifices' of domination is one part of the elaboration of a democratic strategy in this country. As theoretical *and* strategic principles, hegemony and consent are indices of democracy providing both a critique and a strategy for transition.[39]

The understanding of the historical and specifically variable nature of consent as hegemony, involving as it does a non-reductive conception of ideology, designates other terrains for struggle between either the 'Jacobin' form of centralizing party/state or the purely autonomous development of forms of self-management which, in isolation, do not affect the question of state power. 'Consent as hegemony' suggests a new conception of democratic socialist transformation for the West signalling simultaneously our unavoidable presence *within* the integral state and the possibilities and modalities for the transformation of our position there and of its structure. In this context Gramsci's work suggests that we must do more than 'acknowledge' those local, regional and specific forms of struggle – in education, the family, urban planning, local communities, the media, sexual relations, environment and so on – by understanding them as more than peripheral to, or evidence of, 'class' struggle and accepting the regionalization of theory which they demand.

VII. PASSIVE REVOLUTION

The term 'passive revolution' is taken from the Neapolitian Conservative thinker, Vincenzo Cuoco, whose ideas were influential in the early stages of the Italian *Risorgimento* and was originally formulated in order to rationalize necessary reforms for the Italian state without provoking a revolution on the French 'Jacobin' model. It therefore served as a doctrine for the exclusion of mass participation in the formation of the new state, leaving that to the work of an 'enlightened' élite – the bourgeois class. This, for Gramsci was the main reason for the 'fragility' of the Italian liberal state at the beginning of the twentieth century. Because the Italian bourgeoisie came to power only in terms of 'domination' and not in terms of leadership, and therefore of hegemony – as 'rulers' and not as 'leaders' in the combined economic, political, intellectual and moral leadership required for hegemony – the *Risorgimento* was essentially a 'passive' revolution:

The formation of this [ruling] class involved the gradual but continuous absorption, achieved by methods which varied in their effectiveness, of the active elements produced by allied groups – and even those which came from antagonistic groups and seemed irreconcilably hostile. In this sense political leadership became merely an aspect of the function of domination. . . .[40]

Gramsci compares this model to those countries where the bourgeois revolutions had been 'active' and had therefore managed to secure active consent. The most obvious example of this was the French Revolution where, by forming organic links between leaders and led, intellectuals and masses, a 'national-popular collective will' was established, representing the hegemonic moment,

... in which one becomes aware that one's own corporate interests, in their present and future development, transcend the corporate limits of the purely economic class, and can and must become the interests of other subordinate groups too ... it is the phase in which previously germinated ideologies become 'party', come into confrontation and conflict, until only one of them, or at least a single combination of them, tends to prevail ... bringing about not only a unison of economic and political aims, but also intellectual and moral unity, posing all the questions around which the struggle rages not on a corporate but on a 'universal' plane, and thus creating the hegemony of a fundamental social group over a series of subordinate groups.[41]

This is also the moment of the integral state when heterogeneous elements are brought together in a relative unity. But this is not a 'single' moment in time. It is rather a continuous process of the reproduction and maintenance and reproduction of the forms of that unity. Hegemony functions precisely to keep potentially disruptive elements from disturbing the *ensemble* of the integral state by localizing potential crises, constantly restricting them to their 'corporate' positions, preventing the disarticulation of the complex unity of the state. But crises in this unity clearly do occur as Gramsci recognized in the crisis of the Italian liberal state which found itself unable to reconstitute its unity in the face not only of economic transformations of the structure of capital, but also of a complex ideological crisis; defined by Gramsci not as a 'crisis of capitalism' but more as a crisis of identity, authority and representation. It was on these terrains that the ideological force of Mussolini and Fascism was able to constitute itself not as the 'agent' of finance capital but predominantly by intervening at the level of civil society and rearticulating the now disparate forms of ideological cohesion – church, family, father-figure, worker, husband – into the grotesque collage of 'Il Duce', motif of saviour and the strong state.

It is precisely in this context of a *crisis of hegemony* that Gramsci extends the concept of passive revolution beyond the *Risorgimento* and applies it to the constant ability of the dominant class, when faced with a crisis, to reconstitute itself in one form or another. Fascism, for Gramsci, is one form of passive revolution in so far as it neutralizes and channels popular initiative and resolves problems of leadership (hegemony) by transformations 'from above' in favour of the state. Another form of passive revolution was Roosevelt's New Deal which Gramsci suggests in the context of his analysis of 'Americanism and Fordism':

The question of whether Americanism can constitute an historical 'epoch', that is, whether it can determine a gradual evolution of the same type as the 'passive revolution' examined elsewhere and typical of the last century, or whether on the other hand it does not simply represent the molecular accumulation of elements destined to produce an 'explosion', that is, an upheaval on the French pattern.[42]

Historical experience to date tells us that the first formulation was the more correct but in his use of the concept of passive revolution here, Gramsci is adding something to Marx's 1859 *Preface to A Contribution to the Critique of Political Economy* where Marx states, (i) that no social order perishes before all the productive forces for which there is room in it have developed, and (ii) mankind only sets itself such tasks as it can solve. As Christine Buci-Glucksmann has argued, here, as elsewhere in his writings, Gramsci is carrying on that earlier 'revolution against *Capital*' by resisting any mechanistic and deterministic interpretation of these words. In the concept of passive revolution Gramsci is introducing an important consideration which is absent from Marx's *Preface*; the nature and role of the transitional state.[43] Against the determinist implications of Marx's words, Gramsci introduces a theory of the relation of forces (economic, political, politico-military) and insists on the need to distinguish what is organic in any given situation and what is conjunctural, that is, he establishes a space between, say, a long-term crisis provoked by the necessity for the recomposition of capital (the organic) and the specific forms of response to this at particular moments and in particular national situations:

A common error in historico-political analysis consists in an inability to find the correct relation between what is organic and what is conjunctural. This leads to presenting causes as immediately operative which in fact only operate indirectly, or to asserting that the immediate causes are the only effective ones. In the first case there is an excess of 'economism', or doctrinaire pedantry; in the second, an excess of 'ideologism'.[44]

It is in this newly-theorized space between the economy and 'necessary effects' that the concept of passive revolution and a revaluation of the role of the state emerges.

We can see that passive revolution is for Gramsci a historical tendency to which the ruling class will resort in periods of upheaval. It emphasizes the *active* role of the dominant class in perpetually reproducing its hegemony and suggests that it is not only the progressive forces which have to carry out a 'war of position' but that the dominant class is constantly waging this 'war', and that it will always seek a resolution on its own terms, in favour of the existing apparatus. However, this may none the less result in transformations of the relations between classes and the state as has happened in differing ways in all the bourgeois democracies since the nineteen-thirties. And it is from within this perspective that the concept of passive revolution is important for democratic strategy today.

The transformations of capital represented by the crisis of 1929 and the depression of the thirties, and the consolidation of monopoly capital, have all had long-term (organic) effects on the nature and forms of the state in the bourgeois representative democracies. The increase in the forms of fusion between state and monopoly capital (which is not the 'logic of capital') have led, variably, depending on national conjunctures, to an increase in 'economic politics' and a subsequent imbalance between political society and civil society. The state has increasingly had to intervene in areas previously designated 'private' with the resultant politicization of those areas considered as non-political. Civil society is gradually displaced through state penetration into the economy and institutions: the re-organization of the education system, urban planning, the Welfare State, etc., are all responses to a dual and contradictory problem – the requirements of monopoly capital for new forms of organization and a new relation between politics and production and the subsequently increased presence of the masses of the people *within* the state. This poses a dual problem – the response to the presence of the people within the state, and the necessity to prevent them from gaining their autonomy there – and the necessity for an unequal but constant 'war of position' to maintain hegemony.

This process has taken different forms in different national situations and cannot be generalized as the 'effects' of monopoly capital. In Italy, for example, the long period of resistance against the 'strong state' of fascism had its effects in the drafting of the 1945 Constitution which meant that, in the new forms of union organization – the new regional and district assemblies in which communists and militants played a leading role – the 'object' designated the state had radically changed its form. Roosevelt's New Deal and the new forms of corporatism in the USA were a different response to a similar organic crisis. In England nationalization programmes, welfare, education and new ministries were the key areas in which we can see not only 'concessions', but also the negotiated presence of a new relation between masses and institutions.

Since about the sixties, however, there has been evidence that the modalities of this passive revolution have been disturbed, with crises erupting around education, planning, the unions, the media, the role of the family, the role of women, questions of race, the emergence of youth subcultures and so on. The response to these crises has been twofold. First, at the level of political society in England, but more especially in France and West Germany, there has been a gradual erosion of representative government and the increasing centralization of governmental power in executive hands. The power, for example of the Prime Minister and the Cabinet in this country, or the power of the President in France has increased. Where mass social-democratic parties have been in power as in England or West Germany, there has been an increasing separation between the parliamentary group and the rank and file of the parties. Second, at the level of civil society, the response to the 'moral' crises of education, the family, race, youth and so on has taken place on a terrain whose contours are marked out by the populist right of Thatcherism in which she is succeeding in her own passive revolution; Stuart Hall has signalled the failures of the left on this latter terrain.[45]

What is crucial for democratic strategy is that this passive revolution 'from above' be recognized precisely as an active process for the consolidation of the state in increasingly authoritarian forms and that in an integral state this process is not unidimensional from 'above to below' but that we are involved and exist on the terrain where it is happening.

Passive revolution then, as formulated by Gramsci, serves a double purpose here. It indicates that in the *relational* construct of the state the ruling class is operative and active at all levels in the reproduction of its hegemony; that the state is not a monolith to be confronted and seized along with its power. In this sense the concept of passive revolution and the necessary formulation of its opposite – a multiple and differentiated form of struggle for democratic transition, an 'anti-passive revolution'[46] – displaces the sterile reform/revolution dichotomy. This is not one form of *political* transition against another, since its formulation, as opposed to the 'reform or revolution' model, is not located at the level of the received definitions of the political. The analysis of passive revolution/anti-passive revolution concerns the nature of hegemony itself as an active process and the complex nature of the historic bloc. It therefore provides a more adequate basis for the formulation and understanding of the political forms of transition in general and the particular transformations involved in developed capitalism in particular. The combination of the resistance to the passive revolution in political society and the passive revolution in civil society suggests the transformation of representative democracy and the creation of new and diffuse forms of representation on the sites of regional, 'personal', sexual, racial, educational, environmental and local struggles which we have now begun to recognize.

CONCLUSION

In the present conjuncture in Western Europe, we are faced with a number of alternatives which cannot be reduced to the sterile and politically disabling options of 'reform or revolution'. Or rather, it should be part of our task to *create* those alternatives by resisting the simple choices which the 'reform of revolution' model offers us. This is both a political and a theoretical project in the sense that we cannot simply reject the 'models' of strategy which this dichotomy offers: we also have to challenge its discourse and the theoretical (and ultimately political) effects which it constantly reproduces. We would have to start by acknowledging that the dominant forces do not 'stand still', and nor do they necessarily resort to overtly coercive measures. They can find their own *preferred* way out in a passive revolution 'from above' in which they have had plenty of experience in the formulation of complex strategies. The rise of certain forms of 'authoritarian statism' in Western Europe suggest that they are well aware of this (increasing executive power in representative bodies, *Berufsverbot* in West Germany, the establishment of institutional obstacles to popular struggles, such as the Conspiracy Laws or the Criminal Trespass law in this country, Giscard d'Estaing's proposals for an EEC security network, etc.). These measures are not simply 'imposed': they are accompanied very often by an intense ideological struggle waged by the right at the level of 'civil society' where the metaphors 'people versus state intervention', 'people versus power of the Unions', play a major role. In this country we have, in Margaret

Thatcher, one of the most skilled tacticians of this particular struggle with her strategy of 'radical reaction'. The alternative, which is partly in the process of formation in the experience of the mass Western European communist parties and elsewhere, but which largely has to be created, is that we resist this complex strategy first of all by the knowledge that the site of struggle is also *within* the state in the integral sense as Gramsci defines it. And secondly we have to be aware of our presence within the apparatuses and diffuse power relations of hegemony, as complex ideological subjects.

The first acknowledgement, that we are within the state, requires a precise knowledge of the complex historical processes of its formation as an integral state in which we, as subjects, are involved at the intersection of many possible antagonisms, and the rejection of simple models of confrontation – the 'anti-state' of the moment of the Winter Palace – and of the simple models of 'management' of a neutral structure. We still have much to learn from these two moments but it is crucial that we avoid the circularity and closure of options which their discourse reproduces. We need not so much an anti-state as a coherent and protracted *anti-statism* which can both recognize the complex nature of the state and transform not only the 'structures' of political society, but also the power relations and complex modes of subjection in civil society.

The second acknowledgement of the nature of our existence within the state arises from the revaluation of the terrain of civil society as the site of our existence as variably 'consenting' and 'resisting' ideological subjects which are not reducible to the 'masses for manoeuvre' characteristic of much Marxist discourse. This is a combined theoretical and political struggle which could meet the simple demand that first of all we have to *find* the state and then we have to transform it.

NOTES

1. This debate raged throughout the summer in papers and journals too numerous to refer to individually. Its main location, however, was in the journal *L'Espresso* (July, August, 1978) in the PCI daily *L'Unita* and in the left-wing daily *La Reppublica*. See Derek Boothman's concise account of this debate and its implications in 'Italy – the rift between Socialists and Communists', in *Eurored*, no. 9 (*Journal of the West Europe Committee of the Communist Party*).
2. Althusser's critique was first published in *Le Monde* in France after being refused by the PCF paper *L'Humanité* (translation in *New Left Review*, 111 (1978)).

3. See Althusser's 'The Crisis of Marxism', *Marxism Today*, July 1978.
4. Christine Buci-Glucksmann makes this observation in *Gramsci et L'Etat*, Fayard, Paris, 1974, p. 415 (cf. English edition, *Gramsci and the State*, Lawrence and Wishart, 1980, p. 367).
5. Umberto Cerroni, 'Democracy and Socialism' in *Economy and Society*, vol. 7, no. 3, August 1978, p. 280.
6. See Foucault's *History of Sexuality*, Allen Lane, London, 1979. The question of Foucault's relation to Marxism is still unresolved but it is clear that his works such as *Madness and Civilisation, Discipline and Punishment, The Birth of the Clinic* are of major importance for the analysis of power relations and their historical and political emergence in relation to particular state forms. *The History of Sexuality* itself, with its reference in more than a contingent way to bourgeois hegemony and states, suggests at least one fruitful meeting-point of the more recent forms of Marxist analysis with this self-declared 'non-Marxist'.
7. Nicos Poulantzas, *State, Power, Socialism*, NLB, London, 1978 (see especially the section 'Towards a Relational Theory of Power?').
8. Raymond Williams, *Keywords*, Fontana, 1976, pp. 82–7.
9. For a development of this argument see Ernesto Laclau, *Politics and Ideology in Marxist Theory*, NLB, 1977, especially the section 'Fascism and Ideology'.
10. The discontinuities and the 'incompleteness' of a theory of the state in Marx and Engels is argued very cogently by Bob Jessop in his article 'Marx and Engels on the State' in *Politics, Ideology and the State*, Sally Hibbin (ed.), Lawrence and Wishart, London, 1978.
11. Antonio Gramsci, *Selections from Political Writings, 1910–20*, Lawrence and Wishart, London, 1977, pp. 34–7.
12. For this and other formulations on the role of discourse see Foucault's *The Archaeology of Knowledge*, Tavistock, 1974.
13. Rosa Luxemburg, *The Russian Revolution* and *Leninism or Marxism?*, University of Michigan Press, 1961, p. 76.
14. ibid., p. 77.
15. Léon Trotsky, *From the October Revolution to Brest-Litovsk*, cited in Luxemburg, ibid., p. 60.
16. Antonio Gramsci, *Selections from the Prison Notebooks*, edited and translated by Quintin Hoare and Geoffrey Nowell Smith, Lawrence and Wishart, London, 1971, pp. 301–2.
17. ibid., p. 238.
18. ibid., pp. 262–3.
19. ibid., p. 244.
20. Poulantzas, op. cit.
21. In his earlier writings, specifically at the time of the factory councils in Turin, Gramsci remains largely within the problematic of direct democracy/unions/party but he is none the less aware of the complexities of representative democracy and never analyses it purely as a 'class phenomenon' or equates bourgeois democracy with bourgeois dictatorship.
22. Gramsci, *Prison Notebooks*, op. cit., p. 160.
23. ibid., p. 366.
24. Foucault's work on medicine, psychoanalysis, and sexuality demonstrates the various forms of control exercised on the body in specific discourses and indicates that the body itself is a strategic ideological and political field.
25. Gramsci radically complicates this traditional political dichotomy by his analysis of

the 'three moments' of the relations of forces in the analysis of a conjuncture and by his distinction between 'organic' and 'conjunctural' elements (see *Prison Notebooks*, op. cit., pp. 180–5 and p. 178).

26. I would argue that the moment of hegemony in the analysis of the British state dates from the seventeenth century with that complex 'suture' of landowning aristocracy and industrialists (Gramsci), when certain dominant and pervasive cultural and representative forms were negotiated within which even the later working class was accommodated.

27. *Prison Notebooks*, op. cit., pp. 323–6.

28. *History of Sexuality*, op. cit., pp. 101–2.

29. ibid., pp. 93–5.

30. Foucault, *Language, Counter-Memory, Practice*, edited and introduced by D. F. Bouchard, Basil Blackwell, Oxford, 1977, p. 213.

31. ibid., p. 215.

32. *Prison Notebooks*, op. cit., p. 352.

33. ibid., p. 360.

34. ibid., p. 353.

35. For a fuller presentation of this theory of interpellation see Ernesto Laclau, *Politics and Ideology in Marxist Theory*, op. cit.

36. Foucault, *History of Sexuality*, op. cit., p. 125.

37. *Prison Notebooks*, op. cit., pp. 323–6.

38. Poulantzas, *State, Power, Socialism*, op. cit.

39. The work of the Centre for Contemporary Cultural Studies at the University of Birmingham in the areas of culture and domination is one important direction which these forms of analysis have taken.

40. *Prison Notebooks*, op. cit., pp. 58–9.

41. op. cit., pp. 181–2.

42. ibid., pp. 279–80.

43. Christine Buci-Glucksmann, 'State, Transition and Passive Revolution' in *Gramsci and Marxist Theory*, edited and introduced by Chantal Mouffe, Routledge and Kegan Paul, London, 1979.

44. *Prison Notebooks*, op. cit., p. 178.

45. Stuart Hall, *et al.*, *Policing the Crisis*, Macmillan, 1978.

46. This is Buci-Glucksmann's formulation in the article cited above.

SOCIALIST POLITICS AND THE CONDITIONS OF DEMOCRATIC RULE: NOTES ON MARXISM AND STRATEGIES OF DEMOCRATIZATION

Phil Jones

I

Recent years have seen a new creativity in socialist thinking about political strategy. Urgent and often novel problems have been presented to socialists who have attempted to approach them with a freshness of inquiry, frequently accompanied by a respectful but open approach to the difficulties that beset Marxist and other forms of socialist thought. Such creativity is particularly prominent in endeavours to elaborate a strategy of democratization. This involves a concern with bureaucratic and oppressive structures and indicates attempts to open them up through an extension of both representative and more direct forms of control. Such a concern is central to three recent developments. The first is the emergence within the Labour Party of what can be called the Bennite Left. The second is the practice by a whole series of social forces of 'prefigurative politics', and the third is the contribution made by Marxist political theorists in and around the Western European communist parties to elaborate what is often called a revolutionary democratic strategy.

The Bennite left has emerged as an increasingly significant force in the Labour movement. Its principal focus has been on the construction of an Alternative Economic Programme (AEP) which is concerned with democratic planning. Such planning would involve traditional socialist measures, such as the extension of nationalization, but is also concerned to develop planning agreements which make subsidies and funds for investment available only if a firm provides information to trade unions and the government of the day. It is accordingly involved with the fight for workers' control. It sees the necessity to build an extra-parliamentary movement to develop the basis for such a strategy and has campaigned to democratize the Labour Party. Most prominent in such endeavours has been its ostensible leader, Tony Benn, who is closely associated with other Labour Party activists such as Eric Heffer, Michael Meacher, Stuart Holland, Brian Sedgemore and Audrey Wise. Identified with this tendency are a number of key groups like the Institute for Workers Control, the Cambridge Political Economy Group, and Independent Labour Publications with its monthly paper *Labour Leader*. A committee, the Labour Co-ordinating Committee, has been formed around certain of the shared perspectives and it too publishes a paper, the *Labour Activist*.

'Prefigurative politics' is the term Sheila Rowbotham has given to a practice of politics which engages with the present through the creation of co-operative and non-authoritarian forms of organization and intervention.[1] Such a politics demonstrates the possibility of a socialist future by the construction of radical but feasible alternatives in the present. It is to be found principally in the broad range of activities present in the women's movement, but also in movements amongst blacks and anti-racist forces, in environmental campaigns, in local community politics, in struggles around education and health, in the network of 'alternative' newspapers, bookshops, theatres, etc., and in the fight for alternative production plans typified by and inspired by the struggles of the shop stewards' combine committee at Lucas Aerospace.

The practice of prefigurative politics presents a breadth and depth of activities that constitutes an impressive challenge to dominant conceptions of left politics. It demonstrates the paucity of notions of 'extra-parliamentary' activity which reduces it to the pressurizing and lobbying of MPs, and at the same time it develops beyond militant trade unionism that seeks as its sole focus the pursuit of wage struggle. Finally, it challenges the 'technical' character of government and administration, with the mystique of 'professionalism' that so often surrounds it, by the construction of more communal forms of activity.

Both these developments should increasingly demand the attention of wider levels of social and political forces than those active within them. They present a challenge to the existing form of the state and dominant conceptions of socialism. More critically, they point to a form of political practice that is becoming ever more attractive as the conditions have been removed that made both left wing oppositional politics and social democratic revisionism possible political options. Both these forms of political practice sustained themselves on the assumption that economic growth could absorb their demands. As the potential for such growth has been called into question by the economic and political circumstances of the 1970s, so both oppositionism and revisionism have moved into crisis. The consequences are profound, affecting not only political activists but those whose social projects were informed by the assumptions of such a politics. In the present period this has resulted in the formation of a vacuum within left politics so that it has been eclipsed by an anti-statist right. The filling of that vacuum on the left will require the elaboration and construction of practical and feasible strategies and it is these that are signified by the term 'democratization'.

There are, however, a number of problems within such strategic perspectives. The Bennite left, for example, although it recognizes the need to develop extra-parliamentary struggles, is unclear as to how this can be done. It still tends to be exclusively orientated to the Labour Party and, for all its concern with 'democratization', it still remains heavily under the influence of a traditional Labourist statism. Those movements characterized as prefigurative, on the other hand, tend to be largely oppositional in character. Despite the fact that the realization of many of their projects depends on the transformation of existing forms of political and economic organizations, they remain steadfastly antagonistic to operating within the framework of existing political structures. While within each project – law centres, for example, or campaigns around racist laws – there is a recognition of the need to intervene within the state, there has been little concern to generalize a coherent strategy around such interventions. Underlying such a problem is the relationship between autonomous movements and the more programmatically oriented political parties. Such a relationship is frequently fraught with tensions and contradictions, as those concerned with specific campaigns have felt them under attack from the generalizing interests of such political groupings.

Such criticisms are informed by work within the third perspective that has sought to contribute to the development of strategy. Marxist theorists in and around the Western European communist parties have sought to restate and emphasize the centrality of democracy to socialism. In this approach there is a respect for the institutions of representative democracy combined with a desire to extend and enrich such institutions through the creation of more direct and immediate forms of control. The process of extending democracy is seeen as crucial to the transition from capitalism to socialism which is no longer seen as a single and simple break from capitalist social relations but as a complex series of interventions. As such this strategic perspective organizes itself around an attempt to break with insurrectionist and reformist strategies in favour of an engagement within existing institutions and their practices. Such concerns are central to the work of Poulantzas and Miliband, for example, and are evident in the latest version of the programme of the British Communist Party, *The British Road to Socialism* (BRS).[2]

Such work provides a framework which is often more rigorous than the other perspectives. Marxism is a self-consciously analytical body of thought, and even though many of its essential concepts are increasingly vulnerable to sustained interrogation, it nevertheless provides a coherence which no other socialist doctrine has achieved. The work of Poulantzas and Miliband, the programme of the BRS, each accordingly contain significant advances. However, despite the fact that they have broken from the worst aspects of orthodox Marxism, their investigations remain marked by the form of their break from that orthodoxy.

Although there is a recognition of the limits set by democratic conditions of rule on the forms of socialist politics that are possible, there is still a failure fully to come to terms with such limits. Further, whilst there has developed an awareness of the potential for intervention within the state and other social apparatuses, this is often combined with an approach to the economy that refuses any transformation short of a complete rupture. Finally, although existing forms of socialism are increasingly subject to democratic critiques, the implications of such critiques need to be more carefully examined.

II

Poulantzas and Miliband construct their strategic perspective with an interrogation of insurrectionist and reformist strategies. Strategies which envisage the seizure of state power in an insurrectionary dual power situation are seen by them as impossible in the conditions of advanced capitalist democracies. Miliband, for instance, argues that the organizations of the working class have long adapted themselves to, and have indeed been formed within, conditions of democratic or 'normal' politics. Organizational exigencies develop imposing constraints on labour movement organizations, the desire to construct alliances leads to a tempering of demands, and a framework of compromises and concessions is built up to provide a network of ties and obligations. It is difficult, he argues, to conceive of conditions under which that network of constraints would suffer a rupture sufficient to provide the space for insurrection as a strategic option.

Poulantzas argues that insurrectionist strategies are premissed on an inadequate conception of the state, one that reduces it to an instrument in the exclusive possession of the dominant class. It is a view of the state that sees it as a monolithic bloc unaffected by diverse forms of class struggle and which accordingly gives only secondary significance to con- tradictions within the state. Poulantzas locates the democratic state as structured through a complex pattern of class struggles which inscribe themselves in the configuration of its apparatuses. It is a state that is fractured and fissured by contradictions, one that accordingly demands forms of struggle that develop beyond the notion of revolution as a frontal struggle concentrated in a single moment.

Both Miliband and Poulantzas, and the BRS, see it as imperative to construct a democratic road to socialism in which the struggles of the popular masses operate on the internal contradictions of the state. As Poulantzas puts it, the key question within such an approach becomes: 'how is it possible radically to transform the state in such a manner that the extension and deepening of political freedoms and the institution of popular democracy are combined with the unfurling of direct democracy and the mushrooming of self-management bodies'.[3] Such a conception of the democratic road to socialism or Marxist reformism (Miliband) would recognize the limits of constitutionalism defined by the conditions of democratic rule, but would not restrict itself to struggle on the electoral front. It would encompass diverse forms of action within a whole range of arenas as a means to the advancement of specific or general demands.

This is not to be confused with a social democratic approach which it is argued has failed to understand the state. Within the state there is a continued interplay between sites of formal and real power; there is a structure within which through shifts between such sites, reform projects can be frustrated and obstructed. The democratic socialist project according to Poulantzas requires 'the continuous support of a mass movement founded on broad popular alliances. If such a movement . . . is not deployed and active, if the Left does not succeed in arousing one, then nothing will prevent social democratization of the experience; however radical they may be, the various programmes will change little of significance.'[4]

While such an approach is invaluable in the way in which it breaks through the restricting straightjacket imposed by the division of strategy into a series of sterile oppositions, it is beset by a number of problems. There are essentially three problems, each a consequence of the way in which the strategy has been constructed. This has frequently involved the deduction of an ideal typical 'route' that stands between ideal typical representations of revolutionary or reformist strategies. Such strategies are each seen to be inadequate in the general conditions taken to exist in a democratic state or in the general conditions of 'normal' politics. The discussion often then proceeds around the assumption that a left government has been victorious and the problem is then how to deal with the reaction to the implementation of its programme. Consequently although the terms of the problem are transformed, it is still a very classical problem that is being examined, that of the transition from capitalism to socialism, and the conditions under which a capitalist state can be transformed into a socialist state.

The first difficulty that flows from this basic approach is that a left government is seen to be elected at the head of an oppositional alliance, around a new social or political bloc. The second is that, as a consequence of the insistence on mass mobilization, all reforms and programmes tend to be judged on the extent to which they are successful in mobilizing mass action, i.e. on a particular notion of popular involvement. Thirdly, little attention is paid to the specific effects of electoral laws and arrangements and to the specific structures of parliamentary democracies. This is particularly true of Miliband and the BRS.

The first assumption, that a left government will come to power at the head of a new oppositional social bloc, faces the problem that the political conditions that operate so effectively to limit the success of insurrectionist politics operate equally effectively to limit the success of oppositionist politics. Compromises will be constructed, concessions granted, elections will be critically timed; as measures are conceded, certain reforms achieved, others defused, so 'realistic' leaders will tend to emerge with supporting tendencies and the united forces will begin to fragment favouring different elements of the programme. The left, if it remains concerned only with the classical problems of transition, with the conditions of implementation of the socialist programme, would have no strategic orientation to such a situation. It would have constructed the situation such that it would be anticipating a vast popular upsurge and the corresponding coercive response; it would accordingly flounder in the face of an adaptive approach which would incorporate its own demands and engender disunity in its constituent bloc.

To point to the weaknesses in such a scenario is not to argue that diverse social forces should not be united around specific programmes, nor is it to argue that 'left' governments will not be elected; above all it is not to argue that state apparatuses do not function coercively. Rather it is to argue that to pose strategic problems in the militaristic metaphors of revolutionary politics is to obscure the complex processes that are involved. The notion of an oppositional social bloc is part of such a rhetoric. In such a conception of politics, whilst a whole series of radical reform movements are seen as the potential constituency of such a bloc, the significance of such movements is continuously displaced. Such movements are seen to contain the rank and file of such a social bloc, and accordingly the reforms, the demands and the achievements of the various social forces are minimized; they are seen as of agitational value only.

This problem is also a consequence of the notion of mass mobilization that is deployed. A socialist strategy that does not concern itself with problems of popular involvement hardly deserves the prefix socialist. Nevertheless, the language of mass mobilization tends to obscure the diversity of forms and degrees of popular involvement. The notions of mass mobilization that are currently operative on the left tend to evoke images of overt forms of expressive activity along a continuum that ranges from street fighting to mass meetings, with little in between. Such assumptions then provide a model of popular involvement which is invoked as a critique of lesser forms of participation. It produces a form of political calculation that refuses to see how 'intermediate' reforms, which may themselves be insufficient, require as a necessary corollary further reforms the effect of which would be a significant process of transformation.

The forms of participation offered in the Bullock report provide a good example. Perhaps inadequate in themselves, the significance of the measures is that they would require changes at other levels – in the structure of trade union organization, in research practices, in the provision of workers education – which would themselves transform the conditions of workplace and union participation. Or consider the Youth Opportunities Programme of the Manpower Services Commission. Through this programme schemes have been developed that provide means of intervention at a local level that can involve the formation of

cooperative forms of production or distribution. The practices of such
schemes can involve a challenge to the sufficiency of existing educational
and training provision and provides a means of engaging a section of
youth that may otherwise be permanantly estranged from democratic
institutions. There are undoubtedly problems in individual reform
proposals but they need to be assessed as part of a continuum of
cumulative reforms which themselves lead to escalating levels of
involvement, the significance of which is obscured by the rhetoric of mass
mobilization.

The strength of such a rhetoric is surprising. As we have seen, a
constructive approach to the potential of interventionist reforms is
increasingly possible. Instrumentalist notions of the state were one of the
barriers to such an approach, and it is the collapse of such notions that
has led to the collapse of the opposition between revolution and reformist
orientations. Nevertheless, there is often a failure to carry through the
logic of these arguments to an analysis of the economy which still tends to
be regarded as a hermetic entity beyond significant social interventions
short of a complete break with capitalist relations. Accordingly, while
there is a perception of the possibilities open for political and social
reform, this is often accompanied by a refusal to consider anything other
than a total transformation of the economy. Such a transformation
would, however, require the presence of political conditions which, in
their consideration of the state, strategists realize are not present. This is
classically the case with the BRS, but the conceptual problems are best
illustrated through a consideration of the work of Poulantzas.

III

It is not simply rhetoric, however, which prevents socialists considering
the potential of such reforms. There are real structural and political
obstacles that operate to prevent the realization of a wide range of
projects with transformative potential. Such obstacles are in need of clear
and careful investigation in which the conceptual apparatus of Marxism
will doubtless play a vital role. Nevertheless, there are still present in such
an apparatus a series of assumptions that tend to prefigure the results of
such an investigation. Crucial in this context is a notion of the economy
which sees it as a self-regulating machine beyond significant social
interventions short of a complete break with capitalist relations. Such a

notion of the economy is, in fact, problematized by the critical work on the state referred to above.

Consider Poulantzas. It has been seen that he is concerned to provide Marxists with a basis for rejecting the notion that the state is an instrument of one class, that it is a monolithic bloc in the exclusive possession of the dominant class. Such a notion is unable to appreciate situations in which the dominant class does not actually occupy the state apparatus or when the state acquires a degree of independence from the dominant class due to equilibrium in the class struggle, but above all it obscures the extent to which the state is traversed and fissured by class contradictions.

Accordingly he reconceptualizes the state as the 'specific material condensation of a relationship of forces among classes and class fractions', a conceptualization that is meant to convey its character as a set of institutions between and within which there are contradictory sites of power established through the most complex forms of class struggle. Even in the military dictatorships of Portugal, Greece and Spain, the state is seen to have this characteristic. Although the popular masses are physically excluded from certain apparatuses, their presence is nevertheless still pertinent; it shapes the configuration of its apparatuses, affects the policies considered and shifts the relations of force within them.

It is the spaces and possibilities created by the contradictions within democratic states that makes a democratic socialist strategy viable for Poulantzas. In such a strategy popular classes will intervene 'through their trade unions and political forms of representation, but also through their own initiatives within the state itself'.[5] However, it has been argued earlier that Poulantzas still sees such interventions through the rhetoric of the revolutionary politics that he himself disavows. One consequence of this is that he refuses to consider how capitalist relations are themselves subject to 'reformist' intervention.

Consider what is involved in the definition of capitalism. It is a set of social relations in which an agent, the capitalist, has a capacity to sell and possess commodities and enter into contracts to buy and sell commodities (including labour power). This involves two aspects. The first is the recognition of the capitalist for the purposes of the law of property and the law of contract; the second is the effective capacity of the capitalist to control the functioning of the means of production. It should be evident from this definition that such requirements can be met by a considerable variety of conditions; it is not, moreover, a once and for all thing outside the realm of socialist intervention.

Thus it is possible through legislative and other means to transform the conditions under which capitalists hold property and the conditions under which they sell commodities. It is possible, for instance, to construct forms of corporate organization that would operate under a duty to consider the social needs of the community when making investments, to establish an agency to enforce such a duty and to establish forms of workers' control in the running of such a company. It is also possible to specify terms in contract according to which commodities are sold, specifying safety conditions in the manufacture of cars or establishing healthy conditions within which to work. But it is not just legislative reforms that are possible nor just such reforms that are desirable. It is possible to affect the capacity of the capitalist to control the functioning of the means of production. This point is to an extent obvious but its implications are often ignored. Through obstruction, resistance and assorted strategies, it is possible, so it is argued, to set limits to the action of the state. In logic, then, there should be no reason why it isn't possible to set limits to the effective capacity of the capitalist to control the functioning of the means of production. In fact, without such a capacity effective trade unionism would be impossible.

It is increasingly apparent, however, that if it is to remain effective such trade unionism needs to extend beyond the defensive limits within which it has been trapped. In recent years in the development of combine committees, in the work of trade union information centres, through the activities of the Institute for Workers' Control, and in the preparation of alternative production plans such limits are increasingly overcome. Marxism can provide one of the means of analysing the possibilities of such interventions but to do so it must abandon the hitherto dominant practice according to which all elements of the economy are seen as simple manifestations of capitalist social relations.

Under such conditions it should become apparent that capitalist social relations are vulnerable to lesser but more sustained forms of action than those that are concerned with complete overthrow. It will then be possible to develop an appreciation of the potential implicit within a combination of structures; legislative change, cooperative forms of production and workers' control. It is only then that it will be possible to organize around an alternative economic programme not exclusively dependent on state control and thus not dependent on the seizure of the state. Such an 'intermediate' level of demands, it should be added, would in fact require an intensification of the forms and levels of struggle, precisely because they are likely to be more effective.

IV

For socialists to be organized around a series of 'intermediate' demands would be a considerable advance on many kinds of activity with which they have been traditionally associated. It would provide a means of going beyond militant trade union struggles constructed around a limited number of issues but could be related to such struggles in a far more direct way than the propagandistic demands for a maximum programme that socialists have usually operated with. With this Poulantzas, Miliband, and the BRS might agree, but they would be concerned with how such 'intermediate' struggles lead to the realization of socialist objectives.

This raises the problem of what is meant by socialism, a notion that is clearly problematic as a consideration of the range of social and political formations so designated would demonstrate. The Soviet Union, Albania, Czechoslovakia, Tanzania, Yugoslavia, Cuba, Algeria, China and Egypt are but several of a wide range of such formations that would with varying degrees of controversy be called socialist. Each have significant features in common but perhaps at least as significant are the features by which they can be distinguished, features which are due to the conditions within which they emerged, to the tempo of transitions and to existing internal and external conflicts. Further, such states have each and every one been criticized for their denial of both formal and democratic liberties, for suppressing direct forms of democracy, for denying the role of autonomously defined social and political movements, and also for denying anything other than the material aspects of the demands for women's liberation.

Such considerations have enormous implications. Socialists have been happy both to argue that socialism provides the conditions within which the objectives of various groups can be met and at the same time used such demands as a basis from which to subject existing socialism to a critique. The problem lies not so much in the validity of such demands but in the notion that there is a unitary and unproblematic entity called socialism that will provide the conditions within which such objectives can be met. The consequence is that anything that does not live up to the full-blooded image of socialism is then characterized as not being 'socialist' and there is then a refusal to engage in the complexities of political struggle for such conditions are always seen to deny the possibility of 'socialist' struggle.

A discussion of the conception of socialism developed by W. Brus should illustrate the dimensions of the problem.[6] He is critical of statist and market forms of socialism and argues for 'democratic' forms of socialist organization. This would entail a social and political formation within which economic decision-making is devolved, within which there is a high degree of workers' control in the enterprise and within which the forms of political decision-making are also decentralized. Such political decentralization would necessarily involve both freedom of expression and the power to act on the opinions and policies so formed.

Immediately one can see that such a formation would be subject to a series of conflicts and contradictions. A decentralized economic and political system would still require a central coordination but the relations between the decentralized units and the coordinating centre will be one that is subject to tensions. The centre will clearly attempt to set limits to the autonomy of the various sub-groups and the sub-groups will equally attempt to recover any autonomy that has been surrendered for the sake of overall cooordination. This, though, is only the beginning. Such conflicts will not only revolve around the distribution of scarce resources, but will be concerned with the demands of social forces whose identity is defined by their opposition to a diverse range of forms of oppression.

The demands of such groupings are such that to suggest that something called socialism provides the means for their realization is to pose the question in the wrong way. It is more productive, in fact, to face the problem that there is not a single set of social relationships that will guarantee the realization of a series of discrete demands; there is no political formation which will resolve the conflicts and contradictions between the social forces who are currently seen as the constituents of a strategy of democratization. Indeed this is why such strategies emphasize the need for ideological and political pluralism and for such pluralism to be respected within institutions of both direct and representative democracy. In considering the construction of strategy, then, one should consider in any given situation how best to transform existing political, economic and social forms of organization so as best to meet the objectives of the diverse forces in struggle. This is the question that is at stake in capitalist societies, it is equally what will be at stake in socialist societies. Each provide very different conditions of struggle and different objectives are pursued, nevertheless, the point in each is to examine the objectives that are the object of struggle, to examine the conditions of struggle, and to develop a strategy accordingly. Reducing the issues in dispute or the conditions of struggle to the emanations of an essential capitalism or an essential socialism does little to illuminate the problems involved.

V

It has been argued so far that despite the innovative work done by Poulantzas, Miliband and others, the elaboration of a Marxist strategy of democratization is marked by a series of conceptual problems. In so far as the strategies are developed in opposition to models of insurrectionism or reformism they identify certain limits imposed by conditions of democratic rule. Such conditions inhibit the formation of an oppositional bloc that would be the locus of an insurrectionary movement. The formation of such a bloc is still seen, however, as the means by which a left government can be elected without that government entering a social democratic cul-de-sac. It has been argued that democratic conditions can equally operate to disperse such a bloc and that while popular struggle needs to be developed it must be constructed around a series of feasible intermediate objectives.

The potential implicit within such intermediate forms of struggle tends to be obscured by dominant socialist conceptions. They are rendered insignificant by the rhetoric of mass revolutionary struggle which orients itself to and defines its policies by the big moments of political conflict. They are seen to be impotent because they fail effectively to transform an economy which is defined as intrinsically capitalist and consequentially they are seen to have little to do with socialism. It is the form of such considerations that has been challenged in the arguments above. Such arguments are not academic for, as it has been suggested, the assumptions engaged will underpin much of the BRS, for example, and accordingly limit the effects of the advances in that programme.

The BRS develops a clear strategic conception of revolution as a process. It correctly locates the forces for change through such a process in the organizations of the labour movement and amongst a wide range of social and political forces. It identifies weaknesses in each but is concerned to overcome such weaknesses through the construction of a broad democratic alliance. Such an alliance would be one in which the mututal independence, equality and integrity of each of the sectors would be respected, though doubtless each would go through transformations as the alliance developed. The object of the alliance would be the election of a left government around a transformed Labour Party within which the left would have a majority. Such a government would lay the basis for a process of democratization, though steps towards such a process should begin in the present. The left government would fight on a programme that unites the demands of both the labour movement and the wider social and political forces. The success of that programme and the subsequent transitional process would depend on the development of a whole series of struggles both within and outside the state.

This strategic orientation is one that can clearly build on the two perspectives outlined earlier. It can orient to the democratizing current that is organized around the Bennite left and it can develop the potential implicit in the alternative forms of political practice characterized as prefigurative. Accordingly it advances and argues for a particular version of the Alternative Economic Programme and is concerned to elaborate a process of democratization. The problem, however, is that these two elements of the strategy, the fight for the AEP and the elaboration of strategies of democratization – although they are theoretically linked through the notion of the broad democratic alliance – remain distinct, and, in practice, the former, which is linked to traditional practices of the labour movement, tends to suppress the contribution of newer social forces and displaces the concerns of their political practice.

This proposition can be illustrated through an examination of the form of the AEP. This is a programme that depends for its successful realization on the formation of a left government. Given that such a government is not immediately likely to be elected it attempts to connect the long-term objectives of the programme to existing short-term struggles but in a way which is quite significant. The programme is designed as a 'rolling programme' in which a series of demands rolls progressively from one measure to another, the level of demands being escalated as forces become mobilized in its support until finally the government is elected, state power is seized and through a series of incremental steps socialism is eventually achieved.

The programme begins in the current situation where the battle to break incomes policies or develop the wages struggle is given priority. An increase in wages is seen as not only socially necessary, given the problem of low pay and the deterioration in living standards, but will also lead to an increase in investment. If wage rises are then passed on in price increases an effective policy of price controls will be needed. If price controls lead to bankruptcies and stagnation, despite the prognosis of expansion, nationalization and other 'drastic controls' are deployed. Expansion will be assisted by an increase in state expenditure around a programme of social interventions which will be financed through taxes on the rich. If expansion leads to import penetration then import controls will be imposed and so on to the next demand.

In short, as Bill Warren reveals in a series of cryptic comments, through such a development of measures the left which 'no longer relies on an economic crash . . . has developed the do-it-yourself crash, in which you push up monetary wages to raise disruption to the overall accumulation system of capitalism [and] then to bring about the crash of capitalism itself'.[7] There is thus underpinning the strategy of revolution as a process a quite insurrectionist approach to the economy which effectively undermines the notion of a broad democratic alliance constructed in such a process.

Such a notion is undermined because it is the actions of only one section of the alliance, organized trade unionists agitating on the wages front, that effectively requires the implementation of the whole programme. There is thus developed a strategy not of each sector of the alliance elaborating and developing a coherent vision of advance through a fruitful interchange of perspectives, as suggested in the BRS, but of all sectors being forced to fall in behind the vanguard of organized trade unionists, the role of other sectors is essentially that of support.

Curiously such a programme is a mirror image of that advanced within Croslandite revisionism. For Crosland conditions of economic growth would enable private citizens to pursue their life activities, but such conditions would be provided by a benevolent administration. The BRS has a class analysis of such an administration; moreover it recognizes that the Keynesian strategies on which Crosland depended are no longer effective. Nevertheless there is a parallel. The state is now forced through militant trade union action to adopt an expansionist economic programme and it is this expansion that provides the conditions within which the other sections of the broad democratic alliance can pursue their objectives.

What is needed instead of this is a programme that builds upon struggle around a series of intermediate objectives. This would involve, for example, constructing feasible job-creation schemes; it would involve struggling to democratize the enterprise through forms of workers control; it would involve developing price controls which combined legislative with local action. In short it would involve transforming the Alternative Economic Programme of the left from the programme of a sectional movement into the programme of a genuine alliance. This would not necessarily depend for its realization on the election of a left government and it would not depend on mass demonstrations and rallies, rather it would build on the advanced practices developing in the labour movement and amongst new social and political forces. It should be specifically anti-statist in its mechanisms and it should be developed through the construction of alternatives in the localities.

The work of Poulantzas and Miliband has been vital in the development within Marxism of a democratic strategy. A similar contribution has been made by the British Communist Party in its elaboration of a strategic perspective around the formation of a broad democratic alliance. Such work has already led to invaluable developments which have informed wider debates both within and beyond the labour movement. But the contribution that could be made by Marxists developing such work to the ongoing debates on democratization could be greater.

The notion of transition as a process is invaluable, the need to maximize the contributions of both the advanced sectors of the labour movement and the exciting developments within newer social and political forces is clear; they come together in the construction of a series of realizable and feasible demands that are conceived as stepping-stones towards further advances. But the potential implicit in such notions is at the moment only too often suppressed by artificially-constructed notions of transition, by an overarching conception of capitalist social relations and by a notion of socialism that is unproblematically seen to provide the conditions for the realization of all the objectives of the diverse sectors that combine within the broad democratic alliance. If such notions could be overcome the capacity to advance a socialist strategy that is both combative and effective will be greatly increased.

NOTES

1. S. Rowbotham, H. Segal and H. Wainwright, *Beyond the Fragments*, Merlin Press, 1979.

2. N. Poulantzas, *State, Power, Socialism*, New Left Books, 1978; R. Miliband, *Marxism and Politics*, OUP, London, 1977; R. Miliband, 'Constitutionalism and Revisionism: Notes on Eurocommunism', *The Socialist Register*, London, 1979.

3. Poulantzas, op. cit., p. 256.

4. ibid., p. 263.

5. ibid., p. 261.

6. W. Brus, *Socialist Ownership and Political Systems*, Routledge and Kegan Paul, London, 1975.

7. B. Warren, 'Working Class Power: Britain's Crisis', *Problems of Communism*, British and Irish Communist Organization (BICO), p. 22 (Winter 1976); see also J. Lloyd, 'The British Road Debate', *Problems of Communism*, 10 (BICO), (Spring 1978).

POPULAR-DEMOCRATIC
vs
AUTHORITARIAN POPULISM: TWO WAYS OF 'TAKING DEMOCRACY SERIOUSLY'

Stuart Hall

I

The question of democracy ceases to be the subject of abstract speculation, and becomes concrete and politically compelling in the context of the 'crisis of the British state' which now confronts us. Crisis has appeared to be the very condition of existence of the social formation for two decades – some would argue, for nearly a century. But few would deny that, since the political débâcles of 1972 and 1974, and the economic recession after 1975–6, that crisis has reached a qualitatively new stage.[1] The Heath interregnum was a bold, contradictory bid to 'renovate', employing the twin instruments of the economic free-for-all and legal compulsion. It ended in ruins, brought to a conclusion by its internally contradictory twists and by a widening but defensive class militancy. The Callaghan episode – a squalid and disorganizing interlude – restored the now-classical *repertoire* of the social-democratic management of capitalist crisis, but on a markedly weakening political base. As that social-democratic *repertoire* was progressively eroded and exhausted, the fissures in British society became everywhere more manifest. The synchronization of the long-term crisis of the British economy with a world-wide capitalist recession put paid to any prospects (and there were few, even had conditions been more propitious) of the 'regeneration' of economic conditions. In this period, the economic recession began really to bite in one sector after another of social life. The sharp round of wage militancy in the opening months of 1979 was a symptom of stalemate: a strategy of conservative containment confronted by a militant defence of declining living standards; the one unable to constitute the social and political conditions for recovery; the other able only to inflict instant damage in a losing battle against the erosion of real wages by inflationary pressures.

More pertinent to our concerns have been the political and ideological conditions of 'crisis' which this interlude has revealed. The period has witnessed the *de facto* erosion of the two-party dominance of the parliamentary scene, and the opportunist construction of temporary parliamentary coalition, alliances and pacts for the most short-term and pragmatic ends – that patching of cliques and cabals, that wheeling and dealing in the lobbies, which is a sign of the undermining of the representative parliamentary democratic system, and characteristic of the slow drift towards a 'government of national interest'.[2] There have also been the muffled but unmistakable signs of a fragmentation of the national state itself, in the movement towards devolution and regionalization; the first really significant shift of that kind since (excepting Ireland) the Act of Union.

The rotation of parliamentary fractions may not in itself be of structural significance: but it provides symptomatic evidence of a general crisis of political representation. There have been important secular shifts and drifts in the relation between the classes and their traditional means of political representation: that process by which 'the great masses . . . become detached from their traditional ideologies, and no longer believe what they used to believe' which, as Gramsci argued, 'consists precisely in the fact that the old is dying and the new cannot be born'.[3] Coupled with the new forces of the 'radical' right, and the fragmentation of the traditional political ideologies of the social-democratic left, they point, if not to that 'force of non-party men linked to the government by paternalist ties of a Bonapartist-Caesarist type', then at least to a moment of what Gramsci called profound *transformism*, not unjustly referred to as creating the conditions for a 'parliamentary dictatorship'.[4] In this setting, the question of democracy becomes a principal site and stake in the struggle – the very object of the strategies of transformism, from right and left alike. Across this terrain, in the coming period, some of the most decisive engagements in the 'war of position' are destined to be joined.

Everything thus depends on how, in relation to the issue of democracy, the present crisis is understood. It has gradually dawned on the left, face to face with the crisis, that – whatever the classical texts and revolutionary cookbooks prescribe – the possibility that the crisis may now be seized, and shaped so as to create favourable conditions fo. an advance towards socialism, is inextricably linked with the deepening of democratic life, and the widening of popular-democratic struggle. In that way alone lies the possibility of dividing the classes along the line of the exploited and the exploiters, which, in turn, alone might provide the conditions for a more sustained socialist advance. This is the only strategy – leaving theory alone for a moment – relevant to that 'Caesarist' moment, when 'the "lower classes" do not want the old and when the "upper classes" cannot continue in the old way'. About such an unstable equilibrium of forces, Lenin pertinently observed: 'This truth may be expressed in other words: revolution is impossible without a national crisis affecting both the exploited and the exploiters'.[5] Gramsci reminds us that 'A Caesarist solution can exist even without a Caesar. . . . The parliamentary system has also provided a mechanism for such compromise solutions. The "Labour" governments of MacDonald were to a certain degree solutions of this kind.'[6] This kind of alternative could be an extended process, in which 'various gradations of Caesarism succeeded one another, culminating in a more pure and permanent form. . . . Every coalition government is a first stage of Caesarism'. The 'morbid symptoms' which appear in such an interregnum are certainly no longer merely the figments of the fevered imaginations of the ideologues of the far right. The questions for the left here are of both the 'what' and the 'how' variety: in what forms can a popular democracy towards the left (one contrasted with a populist democracy, powerfully inflected towards the right) be advanced? How can an affiliation to the right be checked? And (given its strategic weakness, in the face of this qualitatively new historical task) by what means?

This question has attained a new urgency because, perhaps for the first time in the post-war political history of the British state, the right is also convinced that it/we 'cannot continue in the old way'. This constitutes a quite different, qualitatively new, phase of the conjuncture. For now it is no longer a question of popular-democratic struggle from the left confronting social and political forces committed to the 'defence of the old'. The crisis has taken *both* right and left past its 'passive' point – that point where the political task for the ruling classes is merely to *conserve* the integrity of the state in conditions of economic recession.

The right has thoroughly renovated and 'reformed' itself.[7] It constitutes a political-ideological force of an altogether new kind. And, despite the gestures which the leadership occasionally makes to tradition, it must now be understood as an *active* political force, actively committed to the philosophy that, in order to conserve, it must reform, in order to preserve it must revolutionize. It regards the current crisis as providing, not a passive *status quo* to be defended, but as a strategic political field of force to be reconstructed: reconstructed, of course, to the right. What is more – like the left – it too regards 'democracy', in its *populist* aspect, as the site to be occupied, the stake to be seized. Mr Callaghan was quite correct – even though he does not understand the significance of what he is saying – when he described the trajectory of 'Thatcherism' as a force determined to 'tear the fabric of British society up by the roots'. In this sense, the disposition of political forces on the terrain of the state has been already significantly realigned. It is social democracy which seeks to conserve the state (as well as the 'state of play') and a failing monopoly capitalism. It aims to continue to preside, by pragmatic political engineering, over the political and economic crisis conceived as a permanent passive condition. It is the right – the 'radical' right – which knows that 'things cannot go on in the old way'. The latter has fashioned itself, even on the margins of actual governmental power, into an instrument capable of constructing a new equilibrium, preserving the system only at the cost of radically *transforming it*. What is more, the right knows that, in this process of restoration/revolution, the winning card is the democratic-populist one. It aims to 'win the people' (and *thus* to conserve the representative form of the parliamentary-democratic state) for policies and philosophies designed to transform the democratic content of the state in its actual mode of operation. It therefore intersects with the forces of the left exactly in the strategic field of 'popular-democratic struggle'.

It should be added that this is not exclusively terrain of advantage created by the right, though it is the one on which it has operated most effectively in recent months. It is partly a legacy of the period of failing social democracy itself.[8] In its febrile efforts to master the economic and political struggle to the advantage of state-oriented big capital, social democracy has undertaken its own type of restructuring. This has itself entailed a far-reaching erosion of the democratic elements in political and social life. Social democracy has progressively assumed those postures of pragmatic and creeping authoritarianism, which had, as one of their effects, a gradual suspension of many of the traditional bases of democratic representation and countervailing power; but coupled with their formal preservation, as the means by which a passive popular consent is secured. This double movement – creeping authoritarianism masked by the rituals of formal representation – is what gives a peculiar historical specificity to the present phase of the crisis of the state/crisis of hegemony.[9] Poulantzas has recently described this 'new form of state' as tending towards an 'authoritarian statism': 'namely, intensification of state control over every sphere of economic life combined with radical decline of the institutions of political democracy and with draconian and multiform curtailment of so-called "formal" liberties whose reality is being discovered [presumably, he means, by the left] now that they are going overboard'.[10]

This is an all-too recognizable scenario. What it omits is the steady and unremitting set of operations designed to bind or construct a popular consent into these new forms of statist authoritarianism. It is this element – which introduces into the equation the pivotal issue of 'popular' versus 'populist' democracy – which would lead us to rename the present process as a movement towards 'authoritarian populism'.[11] The rest of this essay is concerned with analysing this phenomenon.

II

Scenarios of 'crisis' have an honoured place in the Marxist tradition but thinking them strategically, conjuncturally, politically has not been a notable area of success. The most extensive work deals with economic conditions and tendencies, theorized across social formations at a very high level of abstraction. Even this work, with the fatalist twist it has so often been given, is now, rightly, regarded as contentious and problematic. In any case, a shift of theoretical perspective is required as soon as one moves from deductions based on an abstracted 'tendency of the rate of profit to fall', etc., to the complex, historically-specific terrain of a crisis which affects – but in uneven ways – a specific national-social formation as a whole.

Certain negative protocols can be established quite quickly. The economic aspects may provide a necessary level of determination, but they *cannot* provide the *sufficient* conditions for determining either the political/ideological forms which the crisis may assume, or the effects of these levels on one another – least of all, the character or overall tendency of their resolution.[12]

It may be ruled out that immediate economic crises of themselves produce fundamental historical events; they can simply create a terrain more favourable to the dissemination of certain modes of thought, and certain ways of posing and resolving the entire subsequent development of national life. . . . The specific question of economic hardship or well-being as a cause of new historical realities is a *partial* aspect of the question of the relations of force, *at the various levels*[13] (our italics).

Gramsci here decisively repudiates that 'economism' which continues to shadow most materialist analyses of 'crisis', and defines the only tenable sense in which 'the economic' can be said to 'determine'. It sets the fundamental economic 'tasks' historically – it cannot prescribe how those are resolved, or even whether they will be resolved. It is not a guarantee of the long-wished-for 'Winter Palace' show-down. This is because there are many more types of 'resolution' than the stark alternatives between the collapse of the walls of Jericho and 'going on in the old way'. But it is also because the possible forms of resolution of a crisis fundamentally depend on the 'relations of force' – that is, they are subject to the limit of the class struggle *at the various levels'*.

In his sketch for an analysis of this aspect of the crisis, Gramsci insists on two fundamental points. First, that 'if the forces which are active in the history of a particular period are to be correctly analysed' then 'it is the problem of the relations between structure and superstructure which must be accurately posed and resolved . . . and the relation between them determined'. Second, that the 'relations of force' are no simple backstop or final court of appeal. They have to be distinguished into their 'various moments or levels' (e.g. Gramsci's 'three moments').[14] There is no guaranteed order of progression between them. Moreover, they have to be thought in their relation to each other, and in their historical specificity. They 'imply each other reciprocally – horizontally and vertically, so to speak – i.e. according to the socio-economic activity (horizontally) and to country (vertically) combining and diverging in various ways. Each of these combinations may be represented by its own organized economic and political expression'.[13]

There are a set of definite analytic protocols sketched here. Crises are 'over-determined in principle'.[16] They cannot be 'read off' from the economic. They are subject to a variety of possible forms of resolution, depending on how the relations of force develop and combine, in particular national societies, under specific conditions. But there is no fixed 'scheme' to be, as they say, applied. Lenin, speaking of 1917, insisted that its pace and trajectory was 'only due to the fact that, as a result of an extremely unique historical situation, absolutely dissimilar currents, absolutely heterogeneous class interests, absolutely contrary political and social strivings have merged in a strikingly 'harmonious' manner. . .'.[17]

This approach underpinned Althusser's seminal – indeed, his most distinctive – theoretical contribution (the 'Contradiction and Over-determination' essay in *For Marx*). This essay represents a theoretical threshold of the first order, deeply Gramscian and Leninist, in the best sense, in its conceptualization, which we cannot afford, now, to fall behind.

> If the general contradiction . . . is sufficient to define the situation when revolution is the 'task of the day', it cannot of its own simple, direct power induce a 'revolutionary situation', nor *a fortiori* a situation of revolutionary rupture and the triumph of the revolution. If this contradiction is to become 'active' in the strong sense, to become a ruptural principle there must be an accumulation of 'circumstances' and 'currents' so that whatever their origin and sense . . . they 'fuse' into a ruptural unity.[18]

Lenin elsewhere remarked that 'History generally, and the history of revolutions in particular, is always richer in content, more varied, more many-sided, more lively and "subtle" than the best parties and the most class conscious vanguards of the most advanced class imagine'.[19] We must, he said, take into account 'the concrete peculiar features which this struggle assumes and inevitably must assume in each separate country in accordance with the peculiar features of its economic, politics, culture, national composition (Ireland, etc.), its colonies, religious divisions, etc.' The task is 'To investigate, study, seek out, divine, grasp that which is specifically national in the concrete manner in which each country approaches the fulfilment of the single international task. . . .'[20] What is true of revolutionary situations applies, *pari passu* for crises of a deep but 'peculiar' kind, where the little matter of the 'revolutionary guarantee' is a worryingly low item on the historical agenda.

We should beware of another tempting deviation. That is the tendency to deduce both the form and the outcome of a 'national crisis' from some *general* theory of the capitalist state, and its inherent general tendencies – of which the 'concrete peculiar features' are mere marginal (i.e. ineffective) qualifications. There is no 'general theory' of the capitalist state, specifiable outside its specific national and historical conditions of existence, from which a national crisis can be deduced or predicted. Of course, a general understanding of the differences, say, between the 'laissez-faire' and the 'interventionist' type of state tells us something of importance: it would be purist to deny this. It tells us something because of its effects. But much depends on how we understand these 'effects'. These differences matter because they affect the role and position of the state. This in turn will have effects on how the political forces are organized and represented, on how the terrain of struggle is constituted, and where the strategic points of application are likely to arise. For example, the augmented role of the state in relation to economic strategies, in an 'interventionist' phase, *must* have effects for how the relations of force at the economic level are constituted, and for how the state intervenes in the economic class struggle. It tells us where to look for the pertinent sites in the terrain of struggle. But it cannot tell us what we are to find there. The key questions about the crisis of the British state and social formation in the 1970s are not deducible from some general theory: either of the interventionist state as the best 'shell for capital';[21] or (worse) from some *a priori* knowledge of its functional necessity. These general expectations are over-ridden − qualitatively transformed − as soon as we supply those further historical determinations which alone permit us to grasp the concrete conjuncture of historically specific societies at specific moments.

Thus the crisis is *not* usefully understood as *the* 'typical' crisis of the 'state of monopoly capital', deduced as to its British particulars. This type of state in Britain has a very specific national history. It was constituted through a set of particular histories. Especially in the transitional period between the 1880s and the 1920s, the 'representative' and the 'interventionist' aspects of the state were combined in distinctively new ways.[22] It has a long lineage, which has already included a whole series of 'crises' and partial 'recoveries', radically national in form. If the reconstruction of the 'peculiarity' of this historical route is now an urgent political and theoretical task, it will not be usefully conducted from *a priori* or transhistorical assumptions.[23] At best we can say that the present crisis is another 'exceptional moment' in the representative/interventionist state; but it appears subject to those conditions of peculiarity which alone provide us with an accurate understanding of the British situation as the object of theoretical speculation and of political transformation. If we must give a date, we would offer the provisional periodization, 'early 1960s to the present'. If this seems a rather long time for a 'conjuncture', it is worth recalling that a conjuncture is not a slice of time, but can only be defined by the accumulation/condensation of contradictions, the fusion or merger – to use Lenin's terms – of 'different currents and circumstances'. It is a 'moment', not a 'period' – 'over-determined in its principle'.

III

Gramsci observed that there can be many 'current situations' within a strategic conjuncture: each marking a shift or a new stage in the relations of force; each 'represented by its own economic and political expression'. We seem to have arrived at precisely such a passage from one stage to another. More significantly, he observed that:

A crisis occurs, sometimes lasting for decades. This exceptional duration means that incurable structural contradictions have revealed themselves . . . and that, despite this, the political forces which are struggling to conserve and defend the existing structure itself are making every effort to cure them, within certain limits and to overcome them.[24]

The crucial point here is that it is not simply the given, passive conditions of crisis which the left has immediately to deal with, but the 'efforts' which different social and political and ideological forces are making to overcome the crisis, 'within certain limits'. Indeed, he goes on,

These incessant and persistent efforts . . . form the terrain of the 'conjunctural', and it is upon this terrain that the forces of opposition organize. These forces seek to demonstrate that the necessary and sufficient conditions exist to make possible, and hence imperative, the accomplishment of certain historical tasks. . . . The demonstration in the last analysis only succeeds and is 'true' if it becomes a new reality, if the forces of opposition triumph; in the immediate, it is developed in a series of ideological, religious, philosophical, political and juridical polemics, whose concreteness can be estimated to the extent to which they are convincing, and shift the existing disposition of social forces.[25]

Our argument turns on these two passages, from which a number of critical points follow:

(1) Gramsci gives the widest scope and reference to the forces which form the basis of a 'conjunctural' terrain of struggle, and to the series of 'polemics', the 'incessant and persistent efforts', undertaken to shift the balance of forces in one direction or another. This could not be further from any residual 'economism'. It must be related to Gramsci's

arguments that this is a type of struggle characterized as a 'war of position'. It takes place where the whole relation of the state to civil society, to 'the people' and to popular struggles, to the individual and to the economic life of society has been thoroughly reorganized, where 'all the elements change'. Such a transformation of the terrain of struggle depends on the following elements: (*a*) the 'internal and international organizational relations of the state become more complex and massive'; (*b*) the Forty-Eightist formula of 'permanent revolution' is expanded and transcended by the formula of 'civil hegemony'; (*c*) 'the massive structures of the modern democracies, both as state organizations and as complexes of associations in civil society, constitute for the art of politics as it were, the "trenches" and permanent fortifications of the front in the war of position'.[26]

(2) It is critical to get the relationship between the 'organic' and the 'conjunctural' features right. Failure to do so leads 'to presenting [structural, organic] causes as immediately operative . . . or to asserting that the immediate causes are the only effective ones'[27] – in short, to that fatal oscillation, so characteristic of many positions of the left today – between 'economism' and 'ideologism'; the graveyard of many a sophisticated 'materialist' analysis, which veers between tactical opportunism and waiting for the 'last instance' to appear.

(3) The nature of a 'success' in a war of position has to be thoroughly reworked. Victory does not consist of the appearance, newly minted, of some total 'world view', or some wholly evolved alternative 'social order', which has been slowly maturing, like a good cheese, in the vaults of the left, to be brought out at the right moment and propelled on to the field of struggle. It can only be understood as *working on the already-given disposition of social forces*, through a wide series of 'polemics'.[28] The aim is to shift the balance of the relations of force into a new disposition; and thereby to begin to constitute a new result: Gramsci's 'new reality'. These 'polemics' must take the given situation, the present disposition of social forces, as their starting-point, the strategic field of their operations: 'an ever-changing terrain for the intervention of the working class'.[29]

(4) However, what Gramsci here says, optimistically, of the 'forces of opposition' must *also* be applied to those social forces which are contending for the mastery of the current situation, but whose 'persistent and incessant efforts' are guided by the philosophy that, in order to conserve, they must reform. Gramsci elsewhere elaborates this idea through four related concepts. The first is that of the dialectical relation,

in any real historical process, between 'revolution/restoration'. 'The problem,' he observes, 'is to see whether in the dialectic "revolution/ restoration" it is revolution or restoration which predominates; for it is certain that in the movement of history there is never any turning back, and that restorations *in toto* do not exist.'[30] The fixed logic of the left, so often tied to the scenario of confrontation/defeat/triumphal victory, is, he adds, 'useful for destruction but not for reconstruction already under way in the very moment of destruction. Destruction is conceived of mechanically, not as destruction/reconstruction'. In fact, as we know, every fundamental period of 'crisis' is *also* a period of 'restructuring'. The question is not why and how things stand still, but what are the prevailing tendencies of the forms of reform/resolution which are beginning to win support. 'Knowing how to find each time the point of progressive equilibrium (in the sense of one's own programme) is the art of the politician . . . really of the politician who has a very precise line with a wide perspective of the future.'[31]

The second related concept is that of 'passive revolution'. This is not Gramsci's proposed programme for the left, but a 'criterion of interpretation' for deciphering the lines of direction and tendency in those epochs 'characterized by complex historical upheavals'. Simply put, the 'passive revolution' designates all those strategies designed to 'put through reforms in order to prevent revolution'. This casts an intense light on the political tendencies of both social democracy and the 'radical right'.

Third, there is Gramsci's attention to the process he called 'transformism'. Transformism describes 'the process whereby the so-called historic left and right parties which emerge from the Risorgimento tended to converge in terms of programme during the years which followed, until there ceased to be any substantive difference between them – especially after the "left" came to power'[32]. Molecular changes of this order 'progressively modify the pre-existing composition of forces, and hence become the matrix of new changes'.[33] This poses in a new way the manner in which the given space of power provides opportunities for intervention and recuperation by emergent political and social forces.

Fourth, there is the question of hegemony, the formation of equilibria and the process of compromises. It should by now be self-evident that, for Gramsci, the question of 'hegemony' is *not* a question of a permanent state of affairs, in which the action of the relations of force is suspended. It is neither a functional requirement of ruling class power, nor a matter, exclusively, of 'ideological consent' or 'cultural influence'.[34] What is in question, is the issue of the 'ethical state': the ceaseless work required to construct a social authority, throughout all the levels of social activity, such that a 'moment of economic, political, intellectual and moral unity' may be secured, sufficient to 'raise the level of the state to a more general plane'.[35] In societies of this type, this *always* requires the most intensive, extensive and unceasing intervention – 'persistent and incessant activities', the 'widest series of polemics', on every plane. It also requires that 'account be taken of those interests and tendencies of the groups over which hegemony is to be exercised' so that 'a certain compromise should be formed'. The formation of compromises, of moments of 'unstable equilibria', and the mobilization of political and social forces to secure and sustain them, is the material substance of political action and movement in such periods. This ought to abolish the delusion that the crisis is merely an inert reflection, in the mirror of politics, of a given set of economic conditions. The field of struggle is defined conjuncturally by *all* those strategies and interventions designed to 'put a new form of hegemony together'. Any countervailing strategy by the left, which has some lower, less ambitious set of objectives as its aim, is condemned to following in the wake of those which really aim to command the field. They are destined to be perpetually defending a position which is being already overrun, responding to last year's 'golden opportunities'. In the 'war of position', though the defensive-offensive tactics in relation to each position has an overall effect, it is overwhelmingly the question of strategic *position* and *disposition* – that is, the struggle for hegemony – which counts, 'in the last instance'.

IV

Against this background we can now turn to the consideration of *three* aspects of the crisis, not widely analysed in the annals of the left, each of which has a definite impact on the question of 'democracy'; each of which shapes the field of struggle so as to *limit* the development of popular-democratic initiatives; each of which, however, constructs 'the people' and 'the popular' into the 'crisis of the state'. We may define these as: (1) The Social-Democratic 'Solution'; (2) The Law and 'Social Order'; (3) The Emergence of 'Authoritarian Populism'.

The *first* deals with the effects, on the working class and on popular and democratic social forces, of the historical fact that, with a brief exception, social democracy has been the 'natural governor' of the crisis. The *second* deals with the ways in which the popular classes have been constructed into a 'popular' ideological force, enlisted to the side of the defence of the 'social order', and the instrumentality of the law, as an 'educative' force, in this process. The *third* deals with the transformation of the field of practical and popular ideologies, so as to construct a 'popular' consent to an authoritarian regime.

I. THE SOCIAL-DEMOCRATIC 'SOLUTION'

The heart of the question here may be summarized in two propositions. The formulation of economic policies and strategies requires a direct intervention by the state in the political class struggle. The form of state intervention has been, characteristically, of a distinctively 'social democratic' kind.

The key strategy employed has been the construction of *corporatist* forms of bargain and compromise, seeking to establish, within the logic and limits of capital, a 'partnership' between the representatives of capital (principally, in the form of the CBI), of labour (principally in the form of the TUC) and the state ('representative of the people'). The aim has been to incorporate these elements, through their means of representation, into the formation of strategies designed to find solutions to the crisis of capital accumulation.[36]

This process of incorporation has had a weak 'representative' and a strong 'interventionist' aspect. To have the working people 'represented' through their leaderships at the centre of policy formation has sometimes held out the hope of their imposing terms more favourable to working-class interests (as happened in the early days of the 'Social Contract', at the formation of the new Labour Government in 1974). This has provided some justification for the ideological construction of the government as the kept mistress of 'overweening trade union power'. But this has had little or no real effect, when the chips were down, on how economic policies were actually formulated or executed. The side which has been effectively accented has been the uses of this corporatist strategy as a basis from which to *discipline the class struggle*.[37] The Labour Government – between 1966 and 1970, and again between 1974 and 1979 – has also played an active ideological role in constructing popular conceptions of the crisis, its causes and conditions, through a series of discourses which classically set 'the unions' against 'the nation', 'the people' against 'the classes', the 'consumer' against 'the producer', the 'sectional interests' of workers against the 'national interest' (and, a subsidiary but potent theme, 'the housewife' and 'the family' against the 'militant trade unionist' – the latter always, of course, a *man*).[38]

In 'corporatist' containment strategies of this kind, social democracy, organized through the trade unions and Labour Party forms of representation, exploits a classically social-democratic conception of the state as the neutral arbiter between the classes. It uses its historic position as the major form of political representation of the working classes. With the brief exception of Mr Heath's first two run-away years, it can also be said with truth – and Mrs Thatcher has not been loathe to say – that, whether 'Labour' or the 'Conservatives' have been at the helm, so far as the political management of the economic class struggle is concerned, it is 'social democracy' which has been effectively 'in command'. It is social democracy, with its Fabian and 'Webbian' traditions of equating socialism with statism,[39] which found itself in the best, most favourable position to 'win' the working classes *for* capitalist economic solutions. (Paradoxically, it has been the brief interludes of Conservative parliamentary rule in which a clearer, more oppositional role for 'labour' became possible.) It is also social democracy, with its commitment to particular forms of state collectivism, and its illusion that, through the mediation of 'Labour in power' it could win 'concessions' *for* the working class (without mobilizing the class) while representing the 'national interest' and defending the logic of capital, which has led the way in the by-passsing of all the organs of popular-democratic power and struggle, including, often, that of the parliamentary institution itself, in the construction of quasi-governmental initiatives, directly linking the state apparatuses to economic strategies.

The 'corporatist' style of Labour governments is one real index of their dominant political tendency. The disorganizing effect on the political and economic struggle – the working classes and their allies *reined in* by the political representatives of 'labour' – has been incalculable. This is the heart of the social democratic 'passive revolution' from above: whereby 'through the legislative intervention of the state, and by means of the corporative organization – relatively far-reaching modifications are being introduced into the country's economic structure in order to accentuate the "plan of production" element; in other words, that socialization and cooperation in the sphere of production are being increased, without, however, touching (at least not going beyond the regulation and control of) individual and group appropriation of profit'.[40]

The monopoly of the state and its policies, in alliance principally with the state-oriented fractions of 'big' capital, by social democracy has opened an effective, alternative space of operations for the 'radical right'. Ditching the last vestiges of its commitment to 'centrist' forms of bargain and compromise with the overthrow of the Heath leadership, the new right has found room for manoeuvre. It has exploited the contradictions in social democracy. It has capitalized the disorganized discontents of the popular classes. It has constructed an alternative 'bloc' organized around the powerful themes of 'anti-statism', 'anti-collectivism', 'anti-creeping socialism' *and* 'anti-the power bloc' (i.e. social democracy in power). This has proved to be an effective and durable, indeed, a formidable political force and 'philosophy' – with, and this is the key point, wide popular appeal.[41]

II. THE LAW AND 'SOCIAL ORDER': LAW-AND-ORDER

The second aspect relates to the increasing reliance on coercive authority and the repressive apparatuses of the state in disciplining the economic and the political struggle, in the context of crisis. The heart of the matter here is that, as social conflicts have sharpened, and the militant defence of living standards has intensified, so the state has come to rely increasingly on its coercive side, and on the educative and disciplining impact of the legal apparatuses.

We have in mind here the extension, over the period, of police power and surveillance of political groups and individuals; the use of the police and legal apparatuses in a wide area of social conflicts; the role of the judicial forces in containing the economic and industrial class struggle; the employment of new judicial instruments – the Industrial Relations Act, legal constraints on picketing and strikes; the extension of the conspiracy charge and political trials; the abuse of *habeas corpus* under a loose definition of 'emergency'. Just as important have been the elaboration of legal and juridical ideas and discourses around the themes of the defence of the state, the protection of the political order from subversion, and their connection with crime as a 'symptom' of moral degeneration and the collapse of the social authority.

The role of the legal apparatuses in containing social and industrial conflict has been widely commented on by the left: but the way public and

popular anxieties about 'the rising rate of crime' have been connected
with the more 'political' aspects has largely escaped attention. Yet it is the
latter which gives the former its 'popular' cutting edge. There is a history
here, which indeed predates the full appearance of the crisis.[42] The 'law
and order' element made its appearance, first, in the early phases of
political polarization in the mid-1960s, directed, in the first instance,
towards targets of a 'non-political' kind, in the traditional sense: the
student movements and counter-cultures of the mid-sixties, the so-called
drift towards 'moral permissiveness', the hedonism of youth, the 'crisis' of
authority and of social values. Gramsci, however, reminded us: 'That
aspect of the modern crisis which is bemoaned as a "wave of
materialism" is related to what is called the "crisis of authority". If the
ruling class has lost its consensus, i.e. is no longer "leading" but only
"dominant", exercising coercive force alone, this means precisely that the
great masses have become detached from their traditional ideologies.' He
added that this idea needed to be completed by some observations on 'the
so-called "problem of the younger generation" – a problem caused by the
"crisis of authority" of the old generations in power'.[43] What was at issue
was, in effect, the fracturing and disruption of 'traditionalist' popular
ideologies. This ideological crisis, however, assumed the form, not of a
deepening critique of traditionalist values, but rather of a rallying of
traditionalist social forces – a crusade in defence of the Old Order. The
'cry from below' for the restoration of moral regulation took, first, the
immediate symptoms of disturbance – rising crime, delinquency, moral
permissiveness – and constructed them, with the help of organized grass-
roots ideological forces, into the scenario of a general 'crisis of the moral
order'. In the later phases, these were connotatively linked with the more
politicized threats, to compose a picture of a social order on the brink of
moral collapse, its enemies proliferating 'within and without'. This is 'the
crisis' experienced at the popular level in the universal, depoliticised,
experiential language of popular morality.

The themes of crime and social delinquency, articulated through the
discourses of popular morality, touch the direct experience, the anxieties
and uncertainties of ordinary people. This has led to a dovetailing of the
'cry for discipline' below into the call for an enforced restoration of social
order and authority 'from above'. This articulation forms the bridge,
between the real material sources of popular discontent, and their
representation, through specific ideological forces and campaigns, as the
general need for a 'disciplined society'. It has, as its principal effect, the

awakening of popular support for a restoration of order through imposition: the basis of a populist 'Law and Order' çampaign. This in turn, has given a wide legitimacy to the tilt of the balance within the operations of the state towards the 'coercive' pole, whilst preserving its popular legitimacy. In this more open recruitment of the legal apparatuses of control – 'the law' in the service of the moral order – popular ideological forces have played an active organizational role. We must include here the 'anti-moral pollution' lobbies, the anti-abortion crusaders, the 'rising crime rate' lobby, the smaller but virulent 'restoration of hanging' propagandists, and above all the role of the police apparatus itself, as an openly-organized ideological force – campaigning in ways hitherto unknown for the extension of police powers, for a stiffening of criminal justice procedures, for the suspension of legal rights, for harsher penalties, tougher sentencing policies and abrasive prison regimes. The key to this aspect of the crisis – a central plank in the drift towards 'exceptional' forms of control for 'exceptional' times – is the power which popular moral ideologies and discourses have in touching real experiences and material conditions, while at the same time articulating them as a 'cry for discipline' from below, which favours the imposition of a regime of moral authoritarianism 'in the name of the people'. It is therefore one of the principal ways in which the dominated classes 'live' the crisis – as a disruption of 'traditional' ways of life, as a breakdown of the traditional landmarks and social values. Its long-term effect, however, is to legitimate the swing towards a more authoritarian regime.

III. THE EMERGENCE OF 'AUTHORITARIAN POPULISM'

This brief discussion of the ways in which the field of popular morality has been re-articulated in a period of crisis around the themes of crime, discipline and social order bring us to the edge of 'authoritarian populism' itself – and to the proper terrain of popular ideological struggle.

Like other fronts in the 'war of position', popular ideologies constitute in time of crisis a peculiarly important and strategic terrain, an arena of active intervention by organized ideological forces. What is at issue here is the transformation of those 'practical ideologies' which make the conditions of life intelligible to the masses, and which exercise a practical and material force by organizing their actions. What is at issue is the production, in conditions of social upheaval, of new kinds of 'common sense'. Gramsci insisted that 'this is not a question of introducing from scratch a scientific form of thought into everyone's life, but of renovating and making "critical" an already existing activity'.[44] Here Gramsci had the ideological interventions of the left in mind. But it must be applied *pari passu* to the ideological initiatives of those social forces struggling to conserve the existing state of things.

In another passage, Gramsci observes that ideological transformation in the field of practical common sense is 'a process of distinction and of change in the relative weight possessed by the elements of the old ideology . . . what was secondary or even incidental becomes of primary importance, it becomes the nucleus of a new doctrinal and ideological ensemble. The old collective will disintegrates into its contradictory elements so that the subordinate elements amongst them can develop socially.'[45] This is to conceive the process of popular ideological struggle on the model of 'deconstruction/reconstruction' – or to put it another way, as the articulation of an ideological field through struggle.

This way of thinking about ideologies as a practical material force has been recently developed in a suggestive and original manner in two recent contributions by Laclau.[46] Briefly, Laclau argues that individual ideological elements have no necessary 'class-belongingness' or class ascription. What matters is (*a*) the particular ways in which these elements are organized together within the logic of different discourses; (*b*) the manner in which these discourses are effectively articulated to and by different class practices. Ideological discourses work through the process of 'recruiting' concrete social individuals through the process of interpellating them as 'discursive subjects'. Different discourses can be organized into an effective hierarchy through their points of condensation, where one interpellated element in a discourse is able connotatively to condense the elements of other discourses into its 'logic' of arrangement. This condensation is accomplished through the connotative resonances between discourses. The internal principle of the articulation of ideological discourses is their connotative and interpellative constitution; but the principle of their active articulation is given by the class struggle, which therefore 'appears' in the field of ideology, not by the permanent class-colonization of a discourse, but by the work entailed in *articulating* these discourses *to* different political class practices. The discourses of 'populism' and of 'democracy', for example, do not belong intrinsically to any single class. They can, as the outcome of particular ideological struggles, be differently articulated in different conditions. The work of ideological struggle is therefore equivalent to the work of articulating/disarticulating discourses from their previously secured position in an ideological field. Laclau argues, further, that, so far as 'popular-democratic' discourses are concerned, these are constructed around a contradiction between 'the people' and the 'power bloc'. If such discourses are to be won to the right, it follows that these contradictions must be effectively neutralized.

There are problems with this suggestive framework.[47] (1) The term 'interpellation' is used ambiguously by Althusser (from whom Laclau derives it), and can be given either a more classical Marxist or a more revisionist psycho-analytic inflexion.[48] Following Lacanian psychoanalysis (from whom Althusser himself borrowed the term, though he was himself ambiguous about the nature of the 'loan'), interpellation is fundamentally the result of the psychoanalytic process by which the 'social subject' is constituted in a series of contradictory subject-positions. In this perspective, the work of ideological inter-pellation is accomplished in 'ideology in general' through the same process by which the subject as such is constituted. Laclau appears instead to use the term to designate how what we might call 'already-formed' social subjects are recruited into subject-positions in the historically-specific discourses of specific social formations. (2) If ideologies do not belong to classes but are articulated to them through ideological struggle, it remains a difficulty to understand what ideologically-free 'class practices' are and how they function. (3) The thesis of the 'non-class belongingness' of ideological elements effectively exploits the theory of the multi-accentuality of signs in discourse, and the fact that, as Volosinov expressed it, 'everything that belongs to ideology has a semiotic value'. But some of Laclau's formulations may lead us to expect the constant formation and reformation of discourses across the ideological field. This takes too little into consideration the fact that the articulation of certain discourses to the practices of particular classes has been secured over long periods. And that, though there is no 'necessary correspondence' between them, 'in all ideological domains' – as Engels once put it – 'tradition forms a great conservative force'.[49] (4) The arena of intervention towards which Laclau's argument points is, especially, that of 'popular-democratic' struggle. Indeed, almost all ideological discourses which do not relate to economic struggles appear to be too-easily subsumed by him into the 'popular democratic' category (are patriarchal ideologies, for example, instances of the 'popular-democratic'?).

The 'people/power bloc' contradiction, which appears at the centre of these discourses form, for Laclau, a more inclusive field of struggle than those which relate to the capital/labour contradiction, and this is the point: here a struggle wider than that of class-against-class can be developed (people/power bloc, oppressed/oppressors), and that way a wider alliance of popular-democratic forces can be 'won' towards socialism. But Laclau's thinking, especially about the 'popular' side of that couplet sometimes appears to reflect the Latin American context in relation to which it was first formulated: it does not take sufficiently into account the role which 'populist' (rather than popular) discourses have played in securing the 'people', through an effective interpellation, to the practices of the dominant classes.

Despite these reservations, the theory lends considerable sophistication to the rudimentary schemas which we earlier derived from Gramsci's work on 'national-popular' and 'common sense'. It follows from this thesis, however, that, in the arena of ideological struggle – to put it facetiously – two can play at the game. Our argument is that the fracturing of many traditional ideologies in the period of the crisis has provided a golden opportunity for the political right, in its 'Thatcherite manifestation' – without benefit of theory, but by instinct (as we are told all good and true Conservatives operate) – to intervene effectively precisely in this area, and to rework and neutralize the people/power bloc contradiction effectively in the direction of an 'authoritarian populism'. As an organized ideological force, 'Thatcherism' has played – long before its actual succession to power – a formative role, articulating the field of popular ideologies sharply to the right. Some of the keys to this success lie in its wide appeal and 'common touch'; its inclusive range of reference (for example, its ability to condense moral, philosophical and social themes, not normally thought of as 'political', within its political discourse); its proven capacity to penetrate the traditional ideological formations of sections of the working class and petty-bourgeoisie; its unremitting 'radicalism' (for instance, it buried the competing positions of the Heathite 'respectable' right without ceremony); its taking up of themes much neglected in competing ideologies.

Its success stands in contrast with its failure to generate a credible economic programme for 'big' monopoly capital, with its built-in reliance on state initiatives and support. However, ideologically, this has given it greater credibility as the champion of 'independent' small capital and the party of the 'little man' against the big battalions of the state. This archetypal petty-bourgeois 'shopkeeper' figure has a well-constituted space in traditional conservative ideologies, if not as a real social category, then certainly as a discursive subject; the enunciative subject of a whole series of conservative 'philosophies'. This interpellation represents the 'respectable' working class, at the centre of the 'Thatcherite' discourses in its traditional petty-bourgeois disguise. It is a rhetorical and discursive operation much employed by the reactionary sections of the popular press, who also seek to interpellate its working-class readers through this construction – and with which Mrs Thatcher and her allies has forged a formidable alliance.

The success of this venture must be seen in the context of what it is replacing and displacing: the fragmentation of many of the traditional 'Us/Them' discourses of the working class (which sustained the people/power bloc contradiction, although in a corporatist form) as a consequence of the disorganizing impact of the 'Social-Democratic Solution' (discussed earlier); the displacement of the alternative Tory 'philosophy' – that associated with the failures of Mr Heath's administration, which played for a time with radical 'populist' themes, but was forced back on to more centrist ideological territory.

It is possible, now, to see the links between this revivalist style of 'authoritarian populism' and the other themes discussed above – the 'Social-Democratic Solution' and the 'Law and Order' crusades. The monopoly by social democracy of the bureaucratic state has enabled the discourses of Thatcherism to condense at the negative pole statism/bureaucracy/social democracy/'creeping collectivism'. Against this representation of the 'power bloc' are counterposed various condensations of possessive individualism/personal initiative/'Thatcherism'/freedom, as the positive pole. It is possible, then, to represent Labour as part of the 'big battalions', ranged against the 'little man' (and his family) oppressed by an inefficient state bureaucracy. Thus, social democracy is aligned with the power bloc, and Mrs Thatcher is out there 'with the people'. This has enabled Thatcherism to neutralize the people/power bloc contradiction.

In the arena of Law and Order, Thatcherism has effectively exploited a traditional space in popular ideologies: the moralism endemic in conservative 'philosophies'. The language of popular morality has no necessary class-belongingness: but it is also true that traditional and uncorrected common sense is a massively conservative force, penetrated thoroughly – as it has been – by religious notions of Good and Evil, by fixed conceptions of the unchanging and unchangeable character of human nature, and by ideas of retributive justice. These are by no means the only moral concepts embedded in popular common sense: for, within its contradictory structure, there are also the ideas of the injustice, of oppression and of exploitation which arise from the 'Us/Them' distribution of power, wealth and prestige.

'Common sense', in this respect, is a contradictory ideological structure, which, though thoroughly formed as a 'product of history',[50] presents itself to popular experience as transhistorical – the bedrock, universal wisdom of the ages. It is 'disjointed and episodic. . .'. It contains 'Stone Age elements and principles of a more advanced science, prejudices from all past phases of history at a local level and intuitions of a future philosophy'. The 'criticism of all previous philosophy . . . has left stratified deposits in popular philosophy'.[51] Traditional common sense can only be raised to a more coherent level through a political intervention, especially in unusual times, when the 'embryonic' conception of a group 'manifests itself in action': otherwise 'this same group has, for reasons of submission and intellectual subordination, adopted a conception which is not its own but is borrowed from another group; and it affirms this conception verbally and believes itself to be following it, because this is the conception which it follows in "normal" times'.[52]

Social democracy, as a political force, has, however, long since abandoned (if it ever had any conception of) a moral-social leadership of this kind over the classes it claims to represent. It has long ago ceased to work the 'good sense' of the class, its 'spontaneous' class instinct, its sense of the world as unjustly divided into the oppressed and the oppressing classes: it has limited itself to making tactically pragmatic accommodation with the most traditionalist and conservative elements in popular morality. It has no conception of the educative and formative function of 'parties' in relation to the 'classes' which they aim to represent – and which, in order to represent, they must first *form*, politically and ideologically.[53] Indeed, the left as a whole, in its one-sided rationalism, has utterly failed to comprehend the necessity to educate the common sense of the common people, in order to constitute a popular bloc, a practical material force, against traditionalist ideas.

But Thatcherism, with its refined populist instinct, has made no such strategic error. Indeed, it has the force of history – that is, the secured correspondences between 'the people' and the 'traditional wisdom of the nation' – to rely on: a field of popular conceptions, in which it has made a series of strategically effective interventions. Those representations of 'the people', of 'the nation', of 'our culture and way of life', of the 'instincts of the ordinary British people', etc., which it ideologically constructs, it can claim not to have *forged* through ideological intervention, but simply to have 'rediscovered', awakened from their deep social-democratic slumber.

The point about popular morality is that it is the most practical material-ideological force amongst the popular classes – the language which, without benefit of training, education, coherent philosophizing, erudition or learning, touches the direct and immediate experience of the class, and has the power to map out the world of problematic social reality in clear and unambiguous moral polarities. It thus has a real concrete grasp on the popular experiences of the class. In periods of social upheaval and change, it provides a moral reference point, which both grasps experience and sorts it into its evaluative categories. Under the right conditions, 'the people' in their traditionalist representation can be condensed as a set of interpellations in discourses which systematically displace political issues into conventional moral absolutes.

Crime is precisely a theme of this kind, which is present in the real experience of the dominated classes as a threat from within to their already limited material resources and 'sense of order'. And when crime is mapped into the wider scenarios of 'moral degeneration' and the crisis of authority and social values, there is no mystery as to why some ordinary people should be actively recruited into crusades for the restoration of 'normal times' – if necessary through a more-than-normal imposition of moral-legal force. That is why the 'Law and Order' theme is not a mere side issue, not a question relating essentially to the control of crime and the system of criminal justice exclusively: why it has become a vibrant general social theme in the discourses of Thatcherism: and why it has served so effectively in generalizing amongst the silent majorities a sense of the need for 'ordinary folk' to stand up in defence of the social order.

'Thatcherism' has worked directly on the terrain of popular ideologies. It has worked their more traditionalist elements systematically in an authoritarian direction. It has constituted, not a discourse but a field of discourses, in which the interpellations of the one summon up and condense a series of others. In the field of education, it has made itself the guardian of the 'return to standards' and of authority in the classroom. Here it has constructed at the centre of its interpellative structure, the figure of the worried parent, facing the harsh realities of a competitive world which does not 'owe his children a living', aiming to secure, not a decent education for all children but an education which will help *his/her* child to 'get on and compete' (here, the condensation with the figure of the possessive individualist): against this figure is set the 'permissive' or radical teacher, the indisciplined school experimenting with the child, the willing employer who constantly discovers that 'children nowadays can't read and write'.

As in the area of crime, these discourses have been elaborated, and gained a hold in the popular universe, by the tactical exploitation of a series of 'moral panics', in which these ideological oppositions are dramatized, set in motion, winning public attention: for example, the intervention at Thameside (Manchester), dramatizing 'the parents' against the state; the well-engineered débâcle at William Tyndale (London), stage-managing the 'parent and the traditional teacher' against the 'radical teacher and the permissive school'. The measure of the success of these and the campaigns of related social forces (for example, the vigorous campaign on discipline waged annually by the conservative wing of the teachers' union) may be found in the fact that whereas, ten years ago, parent-power and parental involvement in the school belonged securely to the discourses of 'permissive education', de-schooling and the libertarian wing, it has now been effectively rearticulated into one of the most potent themes of the 'radical' right – a guarantee that parents will help to restore discipline, authority, traditional values and educational standards in the classroom. Whilst Mr Rhodes Boyson range-rides these populist crusades on the educational frontier, Mr St John Stevas gives them a 'moderate' and respectable voice in the councils of the nation. Once again the link is forged.

On the theme of 'welfare' the outcome of a parallel ideological intervention hardly needs repeating here. The discourse of the 'spendthrift state', recklessly giving wealth the nation has not earned (here, the shopkeeper 'subject' is condensed), and thereby undermining the self-reliance of ordinary people (here, the possessive individual makes his appearance), produces as its discursive opposite the 'welfare scrounger', living off society, never doing a day's work (here, the Protestant Ethic makes a late return) – with more than a hint that this negative he or she is often a 'person from an alien culture' who does not share 'our values' (here, the discourses of race and nation are interpellated). But this discourse also intersects and replicates many of the positions already built into those discourses, which have women, mothers and the family at the centre of their interpellative structure.

Women, mothers and the family have by no means been restricted, in the discourses of Thatcherite populism, to those themes which directly touch on questions of welfare. For women, represented as 'guardians' of the family, are also, by that position, connotatively identified with the keeper of traditional wisdoms, and guardian of conventional popular morality; but this composite 'she' is, at the same time, the 'practical one' – the one who knows the 'value of money' and the 'impact of rising prices in the shops': that is, the figure through which the economic and monetarist themes of Thatcherism can be made to connect with the empirical experience of the everyday life of ordinary folk. 'She' is, of course, the same parent we saw earlier, concerned for the educational chances of her child: the woman alone on the streets at night, who can no longer go about her ordinary business unmolested: the housewife whom the state and the permissive educators would seek to detach from her traditional role and 'force' to 'abandon' her children and hearth and go out to work: and, properly addressed, she is the wife of the militant trade-unionist on strike, who brings home to him the harsh realities and consequences of living without the weekly wage, and urges a 'speedy return to work' – for the sake of the children, of course. Needless to say, she is the emblematic mother of conventional sexual ideology, for whom abortion is a 'crime against nature'. 'She' has played a quite critical ideological role in the construction of popular moralities in the recent period.

In the area of race, 'Thatcherism' has had an even more striking success. It has recuperated to the 'legitimate' terrain of parliamentary politics the extremist racism of the National Front, many of whose basic themes were merged into the official party position on race in an intensive campaign in the early months of 1979, whilst being distanced from their more disreputable associations of street fascism. The history of race and the forging of the political forces of the radical right would bear expanded consideration on their own: the story would have to include the successful 'conforming' of Powellism without Powell, followed by the effective coopting of an anti-immigrant populism by-passing National Front extremism. Here, the interpellations of 'nation', of 'national

cultures/alien cultures', of 'our people', are the respectable signifiers of a
more overt racism. Indeed, there is more than a superficial similarity in
the discursive structure of the two discourses. For the rhetoric of the
Front is also working, not to neutralize but to disarticulate some of the
same contradictions as 'Thatcherism'; and its appeal to 'ordinary, hard-
pressed' people against the conspiracies of the liberal state occupies
something of the same space. The point can be usefully encapsulated in
the report of the anti-fascist slogan (in the business to build alliances),
'Against the bosses, For the blacks', altered by a simply National Front
amendment, to 'Against the bosses, Against the blacks'. The relative
recent decline in the electoral fortunes of the Front should not be too
rapidly welcomed until the full consequences have been considered of
that dialectic between the racism of the 'extremist' and the 'radical' right.

In selecting these three areas of response to the crisis from the political
centre and the right, we have been trying to show that the crisis is not a
given state of things, but an actual field of struggle, on which the forces of
the right have been actively intervening. They are indeed waging a
remorseless struggle, precisely as Gramsci described – through 'a series
of ideological, religious, philosophical, political and juridical polemics' –
whose aim is not simply to conserve and preserve, but to 'shift the
previously existing disposition of social forces'. This is a form of 'passive
revolution'; but if the exercise of social democratic politics through the
exercise of the state had all the makings of a 'passive revolution' from
above, the rigorously *populist* character of the interventions of the radical
right give it the unmistakable stamp of a passive revolution *from below*.
What gives it this character is its unceasing efforts to construct the
movement towards a more authoritarian regime from a massive populist
base. It is 'populist' because it cannot be 'popular-democratic'. This is
what, in the conditions of crisis, the social forces of the right *now* mean by
'taking democracy seriously'.[54]

NOTES

1. For an analysis of this period see S. Hall, J. Clarke, C. Critcher, T. Jefferson and B.
   Roberts, *Policing The Crisis*, Macmillan, 1978.
2. For an original analysis of these and related trends, see Tom Nairn, *The Break-Up of
   Britain*, New Left Books, 1977; and 'The Future of Britain's Crisis', *New Left
   Review*, 113–14, 1979.

3. A. Gramsci, *Selections From The Prison Notebooks* (hereafter PN), Lawrence and Wishart, 1971, p. 276.
4. Gramsci, PN, p. 227.
5. V. I. Lenin, *'Left-Wing' Communism: An Infantile Disorder*, The Little Lenin Library, vol . 16, Martin Lawrence, London, 1934, p. 65.
6. Gramsci, PN, p. 220.
7. For an analysis of the reconstruction of the 'radical right' under the Thatcher leadership, see S. Hall, 'The Great Moving Right Show', *Marxism Today*, January 1979.
8. This question is analysed further below, in the section on 'The Social-Democratic Solution'. But it is worth saying that it still constitutes *the* problem of and for the Left. It cannot be ignored, since social democracy is the political-ideological force which organizes and represents the majority of the working class. Democratic-popular struggles requires the formation of strategic alliances, and hence the question of the character of 'left' social democracy is critical. The disasters of the period of 'social fascism' are too well known to rehearse, or repeat. Yet, without falling into an essentialist conception of social democracy, it condenses within itself all the problems which 'reformism' constitute for any radical transformation. This is accentuated in the period when social democracy in power becomes, effectively, the 'natural' manager of the capitalist crisis.
9. It is also what distinguished this phase of the crisis from any simple reduction to 'fascism'.
10. N. Poulantzas, *State, Power, Socialism*, New Left Books, 1978, pp. 203–4.
11. For a definition of 'authoritarian populism', see S. Hall, op. cit., 1979.
12. The neglect of this 'necessary sufficient' distinction has confused many of the recent debates concerning 'determination by the economic'. Despite Marx's observation that the concrete is the result of 'many determinations', and Althusser's concept of 'over-determination', it continues to be argued that logically the economic must either determine, or not; but it cannot be 'relatively determinate'. But relations are never so either/or as this logical binary suggests in the 'logic of historical process'.
13. Gramsci, PN, p. 184.
14. Gramsci, PN, pp. 177ff.
15. ibid., pp. 180–2.
16. L. Althusser, 'Contradiction and Overdetermination', *For Marx*, Allen Lane, Penguin, 1969, p. 101.
17. Lenin, *Letters From Afar*, No. I, pp. 35–6; quoted in Althusser, op. cit., p. 99.
18. Althusser, ibid., p. 99.
19. Lenin, *Left-Wing Communism*, p. 75.
20. Lenin, ibid., pp. 72–3.
21. For a lucid discussion of this formulation, see B. Jessop, 'Capitalism And Democracy: The Best Possible Shell?' in *Power and the State*, ed. Littlejohn, Smart, Wakeford and Yuval-Davis, Croom Helm, 1978.
22. In this version of the paper, I have omitted a long discussion of the relation between the 'representative' and 'interventionist' elements of the modern capitalist state, especially in the new forms of their combination in the 1880–1920 period. It suffices to say here that these two aspects must now be distributed as between their 'good' and 'bad' side: they are complementary and contradictory features of many variants of state and of specific political regimes after the 'transition to monopoly' begins.
23. The reconstruction of the emergence of this state form in British conditions *is* indeed an urgent theoretical-political task now for the left.

24. Gramsci, PN, p. 178.
25. ibid.
26. These elements of the phase of 'war of position' form part of Gramsci's seminal discussion, in PN, pp. 242–3.
27. Gramsci, PN, p. 178.
28. It is sometimes thought that to speak of 'working on the already-given disposition of social forces' is next-door to succumbing to a reformist strategy. This is the product of that 'optimism/fatalism' oscillation, which besets the left in periods of containment, which Gramsci has so pertinently analysed. In fact, nothing could be farther from the truth.
29. For this quote, and a thoughtful and suggestive outline of Gramsci's political thinking, see Anne Sassoon, 'Hegemony and Political Intervention', in *Politics, Ideology and The State*, CUL Papers, Lawrence and Wishart, 1978, edited by S. Hibbin.
30. Gramsci, PN, p. 219.
31. Quoted from Gramsci's *Quaderni*, p. 1825, in Sassoon, op. cit., p. 24.
32. Gramsci, PN, p. 58.
33. Gramsci, PN, p. 109.
34. For an extended argument on this point, see Hall, Lumley and McLennan, 'Politics and Ideology in Gramsci', in *On Ideology*, Hutchinsons and Centre for Cultural Studies, 1978.
35. Gramsci, PN, pp. 181–2.
36. Perhaps it needs to be stressed that the 'means of political representation' do not automatically reflect an already-formed, homogeneous class, with ascribed 'class interests' and a formed coherent 'world view', outside the representation process. Representation is an active and formative relation between 'parties' and 'classes': they *form* and constitute 'the class' politically and ideologically by representing it. However, *a propos* the argument that there can only be 'means of representation' and 'what is represented', we would argue that there must be something there to be 'represented', even if it is altered and transformed in the process.
37. See the discussion in S. Hall, *et al.*, *Policing The Crisis*, Part IV.
38. The heart of the Social-Democratic representation of the working class and its allies is the displacement of the 'representative' relation (in the articulation 'class-party') into the disciplinary-interventionist articulation, 'party-nation'. For a discussion of this aspect, see S. Hall, 'Newspapers, Parties and Classes', in *The British Press: A Manifesto*, ed. J. Curran, Macmillan, 1978; and 'Social Democracy, Education and the Crisis', Finn, Grant and Johnson, in *On Ideology*, op. cit.
39. The complex relations between 'Liberal Collectivism' and Fabian Social-Democratic statism is currently the subject of an extensive reworking by the 'new liberal' school of historians, but is of the utmost importance to a Left analysis of the character of British Social Democracy and of the British state. Cf., *inter alia*, Emy, *Liberals, Radicals and Social Politics*, Cambridge, 1973; P. Clarke, *Liberals and Social-Democrats*, Cambridge, 1979.
40. Gramsci, PN, p. 120.
41. See S. Hall, 'The Great Moving Right Show', op. cit., 1979.
42. For the history of the slow drift to a 'law and order' state, see S. Hall, *et al.*, *Policing The Crisis*, 1978.
43. Gramsci, PN, pp. 276–7.
44. Gramsci, PN, p. 330.
45. From Gramsci, *Quaderni*, III, p. 1875, quoted in the context of a lucid and

exemplary discussion of Gramsci's conception of ideology, in the introductory essay, by Chantal Mouffe, to a forthcoming selection of essays on Gramsci's work. I have greatly benefited from an opportunity to see this essay before publication.

46. Ernesto Laclau, *Politics and Ideology in Marxist Theory*, New Left Books, 1977; an elegant and original contribution to Marxist theory.

47. I am indebted, in formulating some of these criticisms, to the paper 'Laclau and Interpellation' by Alan O'Shea: Centre for Cultural Studies, Birmingham mimeo, 1978.

48. In Althusser's influential essay, 'Ideology and Ideological State Apparatuses', *Lenin and Philosophy and Other Essays*, New Left Books, 1971. These were originally two essays, revised into a single text; but the two parts are still visible: the first relates ideology to the reproduction of the relations of production and to hegemony; the second argues that ideology requires the constitution of 'subjects', through interpellation. The term is borrowed from Lacan, and is the theoretical warrant for much subsequent theorizing attempting to combine Marxism with Lacanian psychoanalysis. Althusser's usage here is, however, highly ambiguous – and one is tempted to think not unconsciously so, for the volume also contains the important 'Freud and Lacan' essay. Althusser's tentative formulation, that 'the eternity of the unconscious is not unrelated to the eternity of ideology in general' (p. 152) has since lost all qualifications in the assertion that ideology *is* structured like, and acquired in the same process that constitutes the unconscious. For some continuing problems with this assertion, see S. Hall, 'Some Problems with the Ideology/Subject Couplet' and the Editorial Reply, in *Ideology and Consciousness*, No. 3. Spring 1978.

49. Engels, 'Feuerbach and the End of Classical German Philosophy', in *Marx-Engels Selected Works*, vol. 2, Lawrence and Wishart, 1951, p. 362.

50. Gramsci, PN, p. 325.

51. Gramsci, PN, p. 324.

52. Gramsci, PN, p. 327.

53. See above, footnote 36.

54. In its recent conversion to the strategy of 'alliances' and 'popular-democratic' struggle, the left – freed of the essentialism of some of its old, sectarian, 'reformism/revolution' binarism – sometimes acts and talks as if only *it* is in a position to seize the 'democratic-popular' initiative. This article is written in the conviction that the right also knows how to 'take democracy seriously', and may have been more effective than the left in doing so – in a certain way. It is now also sometimes argued that, in the search for 'openings' the left should cease asking the question about 'reformism'. This seems to me a damaging evacuation. There is no necessary, permanent, inevitable essential content to be ascribed to 'reformism': it can only be defined in the conjuncture, in relation to the balance of forces. But the crucial question, as to whether any strategy is working on a pertinent contradiction (in such a way that it cannot be resolved without transformation) or so as to 'permit reforms which do not touch the essential structure', remains in my view an extremely pertinent political question to ask – of any intervention or any alliance. We may have abandoned the fixed ascription of reformism as a pejorative label. Unfortunately, the political *problem* of reformism is still very much present.

NOTES ON CONTRIBUTORS

Alan Hunt is Assistant-Dean at Middlesex Polytechnic. He edited *Class and Class Structure*, Lawrence and Wishart, 1977, and has written *The Sociological Movement in Law*, Macmillan, 1978 and (with Maureen Cain) *Marx and Engels on Law*, Academic Press, 1979. He is Secretary of the Sociology Group of the Communist Party.

Barry Hindess is Senior Lecturer in Sociology at the University of Liverpool. His most recent publications have been: *Mode of Production and Social Formation* (with Paul Hirst), Routledge and Kegan Paul, 1977; *Philosophy and Methodology in the Social Sciences*, Harvester, 1977; and (with A. Cutler, P. Hirst and A. Hussain) *Marx's Capital and Capitalism Today*, 2 vols, Routledge and Kegan Paul, 1977/8.

Bob Jessop is a lecturer in government at the University of Essex; he has published a number of articles on state theory, democracy and corporatism; his book *Theories of the Capitalist State* will be published by Martin Robertson in 1980.

Anne Showstock Sassoon is Senior Lecturer in Politics at Kingston Polytechnic. She studied at the University of California, Berkeley, the University of Padua, and at the London School of Economics. She has published a number of articles on Gramsci, and her forthcoming book, *Gramsci's Politics* will be published by Croom Helm.

Colin Mercer is a research assistant at the Open University (Faculty of Arts) working on the Marxist theory of ideology. He is a member of the editorial collective of *Red Letters*.

Phil Jones is a Senior Lecturer in the Department of Law at the Polytechnic of Central London.

Stuart Hall is Professor of Sociology at the Open University; he was previously Director of the Centre for Contemporary Cultural Studies at the University of Birmingham. He has published widely in the fields of race, youth culture, media studies and Marxist theory and politics. He is co-author of *Policing The Crisis*, Macmillan, 1978.

INDEX